Sports Writing
A Beginner's Guide

By Steve Craig

Discover Writing Press
PO Box 264
Shoreham, VT 05770
1-800-613-8055
fax # 802-897-2084
www.discoverwriting.com

Copyright © 2002 by Steve Craig
ISBN # 0-9656574-9-3
Library of Congress control number 00 092517

Cover Design by Jim Burns
Photos by Mark Bolton
Special thanks to Foster's Daily Democrat for use of articles on the cover.

All rights reserved. No part of this work may be reproduced or transmitted in any form or by any means, electronic or mechanical, including photocopying and recording, or by any information storage or retrieval system, except as may be expressly permitted by the 1976 Copyright Act or in writing by the publisher, or for the purchaser's own personal use in the classroom.

Every effort has been made to contact the students and copyright holders to reprint borrowed material. We regret any oversights that may have occurred and would be happy to rectify them in future printings of this work.

> For information about writing seminars call Discover Writing Company 1-800-613-8055 or visit our website: www.discoverwriting.com

For all my teachers,
especially Debby, Martha Jane, Claire and John D.

Contents

Introduction 1

Chapter 1: There's More to Journalism than Writing 5

Chapter 2: Fact vs. Fiction 17

Chapter 3: Getting the Facts and Getting Them Straight 27

Chapter 4: The Interview 43

Chapter 5: Writing the Story 61

Chapter 6: Game Stories 71

Chapter 7: The Feature Story 91

Chapter 8: What is a Sidebar Story? 113

Chapter 9: The Beat Writer's Notebook 119

Chapter 10: The Column 131

Chapter 11: Little Things Mean a Lot 141

Chapter 12: It's Sports Business Now 153

INTRODUCTION

You Don't Have to Play the Game

If you love to play sports or love reading about sports, then you understand the excitement that an athletic contest can create. When men or women put their bodies and minds to a physical test it can, at the highest levels of competition, create a fire of inspiration so great as to demand an entire country's attention.

In this way, sports excite you. Whether in the backyard or the local youth leagues, most of us have enjoyed pretending to be playing the games we love in front of huge crowds and rows of television cameras. I sure did. My friends and I would routinely include our own invented play-by-play announcing and would even conduct "interviews" like those we had seen on television.

In junior high and high school there are plenty of opportunities to actually play your favorite sports and to test your skills in a competitive environment and that's great. Did you ever wonder though, even for just a moment, "How am I going to keep sports a part of my life when I'm an adult?"

For a very lucky and extremely talented few, the answer will be professional sports. The rest of us will play a few years of softball, basketball or soccer in adult recreation leagues but chances are we'll never quite find that thrill and competitive zest we so easily captured as a kid.

What we need is to find a way to stay in the game without actually playing. That's where this book can help and it doesn't matter whether you're a man or woman, a boy or girl. Anyone can become a sportswriter—and **sports writing can be your ticket to get into the game, complete with a privileged point of view.**

Sportswriters are the people who record the deeds, actions, athletes and vital information of athletic competitions. Sports writing has a history that can be traced back for at least 3,000 years.

If you have even the slightest interest in athletics, chances are sportswriters (and their television cousins, sportscasters) have already had an impact on you. They are the people who bring you much of the information about not only your favorite professional athletes but also about the kid down the street who plays for the local high school football or field hockey team.

This book will show you how to get started on a new career in athletics. The best part is, it can be a career for a lifetime—and one you can get started on right now.

Plenty of sportswriters have started professionally before they were out of high school, working for their local newspaper as a part-time employee, either writing short stories or helping with the many other parts of putting together a complete sports section. If you can land a job like this, you can get the always-valuable "on-the-job" experience long before you even get to college or have to worry about getting a "real" job. Plus, unlike the athletes you cover, you won't have to worry about career-ending injuries.

Perhaps the best part is, you can keep getting better, day after day, year after year. Twenty-year veterans in sports writing are often just beginning to produce their best work. As long as they still have a passion for the job, their increased knowledge of sports and people will translate into better writing—and a more successful career.

The more you learn, the more you see, the more valuable you become as a writer.

Like the athletes we cover, sportswriters need a good, solid grounding in the fundamental skills and plenty of opportunities to practice those skills in order to have a chance to succeed. Then qualities like hard work, perseverance, talent, and confidence take over. Perhaps most important to determining long-term success is waking up each morning with a daily thirst for meeting people, discussing issues and writing about them.

This brings me to a personal opinion that is at the heart of this book. **To be a good sportswriter, you need to like people more than you like sports.** It's a concept that really shouldn't be surprising. People are what sports are about. Still, as has already been suggested, most people who are drawn to sports writing as a career are initially excited by the drama and excitement of the games, regardless of who is playing.

What this points to is one of the very few prerequisites to being a sportswriter. When you first decide to be a sportswriter you do not have to be a good writer. You don't even need to know that much about sports. You do, however, need to enjoy meeting and being around new people on a regular basis. It's the people who will help you to learn more about the sports that you are watching and writing about.

Some of these same people will also become your best gauges for when a story has been well written. Most of all, the sportswriter needs to learn how to be comfortable, confident and competent when meeting new people. Whether it's a casual introduction or a formal interview, these first impressions will be important. You can never be sure when a chance acquaintance or a brief interview might pave the way for another story. In the language of the newsroom, it's called cultivating contacts. It's all about knowing whom to call and when to call them, or, at the very least, knowing whom to call who can tell you whom to call.

Again, it all revolves around people. The circle of people that revolves around sports—and therefore can be worthwhile for a reporter to know—extends far beyond the rather small confines of the playing field itself. The athletes will still be at the core of most of your stories but increasingly there are other people who influence the outcome of sports. Coaches, referees, athletic directors, mothers, fathers, doctors, law enforcement officials, community leaders and politicians all can have a significant role in sports. When it comes to professional sports, there are times when the owners, coaches and administrators actually become more of the story than the athletes. As a sportswriter you better be able to talk to businessmen and businesswomen about the effects of a multi-million dollar salary on team dynamics as comfortably as you talk with a basketball coach about the plusses and minuses of a trapping zone defense.

The focus of this book is on the fundamental skills needed to report and write about sports. It will use realistic examples of what a beginning sportswriter is likely to face to help describe what it is really like to be both a journalist and a sportswriter. The book will highlight the best parts of the job as well as the tough parts. This book will *not* make you into an overnight sensation. It *will* give you insight into the real world of sports journalism. It will provide you with the tools needed to start writing—the tools you need to stay in the game.

CHAPTER 1

There's More to Journalism than Writing

Sports writing. It sounds easy. It also sounds like a great job. Go to games, eat some food, have a soda, maybe get a suntan, see in person the professional stars you've been watching on the television, write up a little story, and—best of all—get paid.

Many times during my 12 years as a sportswriter for a small daily newspaper in New Hampshire, good-natured fans or acquaintances would slide up to me and say, "You have a great job," or "Geez, how do I get your job?"

They're right. It is a great job. Writing about sports is not, however, as easy and carefree as I always felt most of these people believed it to be. Being a sportswriter is a job. To excel takes effort, just as in any other profession.

They were right about one thing, though. There are some great benefits to this job. No doubt about it. It's just important to remember that the perks are balanced by reality.

Yes, you do get to see plenty of games, though when you start few will be of the professional, televised variety (unless you're very lucky and very talented). Each summer you do get a nice tan—on your arms and face at least. You will get paid. Sometimes the food is even free. But, unless you're the Ken Griffey Jr. of writers, it's not easy. Writing is work. Getting the information needed to write—by the time-honored means of reporting, researching and interviewing—is even more work.

There's More to Being a Sportswriter than Writing

Sportswriters are also reporters. Reporters gather the news, the names, and details of the sporting events they cover and then write a report (a story) which appears in a newspaper or, in the modern world, on a website. Reporting is the most important aspect of any type of journalism. Bringing new information to the reader and relating it in an accurate manner should be goals that are achieved with each story.

Chapters 2, 3 and 4 focus directly on the reporting, researching and interviewing skills a beginning sportswriter will need to learn and practice. The intent of this beginning chapter is to make it crystal clear that **how well a sportswriter gathers information—the act of reporting—will determine how good any sports story can be.**

Unfortunately some sportswriters, especially those just getting started in the field, too often overlook the *reporting** component of their story. Why? There are several specific reasons, some of which I'll address later in this chapter. The general reason is simply that sportswriters tend to be a creative group when it comes to their writing and sports pages often allow a greater degree of freedom when it comes to issues of writing style. It's the old, "give somebody an inch and they'll take a mile" expression at work.

When reading articles by the best sportswriters in the country you are, in my opinion, reading some of the best *non-fiction* writers around. Their stories are so vivid and well crafted that the reader quickly becomes interested in the story. The inexperienced sportswriter, recognizing that the genre allows a little bit of freedom to experiment and be clever, often tends to take things too far. That's OK.

Writing about sports, just like playing a sport, is a learning

> ### *Remember to read*
>
> *What delights the sports section reader is how well the majority of the stories are written. A good suggestion for any beginning sportswriter is to read as much as possible. Treat yourself and try to read the best. Certainly top-level sports writing (*Sports Illustrated *and large-city newspapers which can now be read anywhere thanks to the wonders of the internet) should be read as often as possible. Don't stop there, however. Read the classics. Read your mother's paperback novels. Read some historical non-fiction accounts of great human events. Read about topics that are not related to sports. Try to recognize how great (and less-than-great) writers organize their information and the way they choose just the right word to describe emotions and paint an image of the surroundings. Expose your brain to the written word.*

---

* Throughout this book, words or phrases that are bold-faced and italicized are defined.

process. Sometimes you just have to swing for the fence. The important thing is to be able to learn from your mistakes. If you strike out with a story, then learn to cut back on your writing style until you've begun to hit the target on a consistent basis.

Plus, in the real world of newspapers there are sports editors who are in charge of sportswriters. Like a coach, they determine much of what a young sportswriter is allowed to do and will then judge the effort and offer suggestions on how to improve. Another thing a sports editor will probably do, at least at some point, is to remind the young sportswriter that he or she is spending too much time writing and not enough time gathering the facts, opinions and details that really make a sports page lively and interesting.

Remember that the really good writers didn't spend all their time writing. Their best stories all started with a huge accumulation of materials, quotes, insights and layer upon layer of background information.

An Example of Reporting vs. Writing Time

For nine consecutive years I covered the local college football team. I literally wrote several hundred stories about the University of New Hampshire football team in that time. That's a lot of time spent in front of a computer. Not as much time, however, as was spent outside of the office getting the information that would form those stories.

Here's an example that will illustrate a typical game-day work schedule, as well as pointing out reporting time spent on the days leading up to the game.

The game starts Saturday at 12:30 p.m. You've been assigned three stories to write for the Sunday edition: A *game story* which details which team won and how it happened; a *sidebar* on the key play, player or theme; and a short story called a *notebook* about things like injuries, who played well, who surprised, with possibly a humorous anecdote.

It sounds like a lot to write and it is. Even a speedy, experienced writer would like to have at least two-and-a-half hours to write that much material, figuring an hour for the game story, a little less for the sidebar, a half-hour for the notes and 10 minutes to pace around the desk, get a soda, and use the bathroom at least once.

How much time did you spend preparing to write? Well, since you are a good solid reporter, you've been to practice at least once, probably twice during the week, and talked to the coaches before the game. Now much of that material would have been used for stories you wrote for Friday and Saturday's papers that served to preview the game for your readers. Still, the knowledge you've learned during the week is information you can—and should—use on game day. So there's a chunk of at least three hours of reporting time, probably more, and it isn't even Saturday yet. On game day, you probably get to the site at least an hour early. If traffic and parking are potential problems, then you should get to the game even earlier to make sure you are not caught in a mad rush before the opening kickoff. This is the time when—between bites of the free doughnuts and slurps from the free soda (see, there are perks to the job)—good reporters are doing some really critical work that can make their stories significantly more informed. The reporter is checking on the starting lineups to see which players are injured, talking to a representative from the visiting team to find out what has been going right and wrong for them, and sneaking a last clue from a talkative assistant coach. This can be important stage-setting material. Do the patterns and tendencies continue? Or, did one team stop another's strength? There's another hour, at least, spent reporting.

Now the game starts. College football usually takes three hours to complete. Of course during the game a reporter should be paying close attention and taking notes on what is happening during the game (I'll talk about specific game-day note-taking styles in Chapter 6). Most keep their own play-by-play descriptions. Many sports reporters will do some writing on their laptop computers during halftime and commercial breaks but you have to be careful not to get too carried away. For one thing, the key theme of the game often is not determined until the final minutes. Also, you need to be watching what you're reporting on closely. There are newsworthy items that happen throughout a game and if your face is buried in the computer screen, they can be missed. During a game a reporter is consciously and sometimes almost subconsciously asking dozens of internal questions.

- Were there any injuries? How much did they impact the game?
- How did the rookie quarterback perform?
- Did the defense play better this week?
- Why did the coach call a running play on third-and-eight?
- I wonder if there are any doughnuts left?
- Is this the most yards a certain running back has ever gained? Were there any school records set?
- Will this team ever find a legitimate field goal kicker?

These questions won't lead to solving world hunger or getting a lasting peace treaty in the Middle East but they can make a sports story more informed.

Now the game is over. You've spent at least seven hours reporting and preparing but you're still not ready to start writing. Now is the time to get the reaction of players and coaches to the game, to get the final answers or interpretations to those questions you were pondering.

This is Interview Time. For sportswriters, it is their personal fourth-quarter drive for the winning material. Comments from the players and coaches are essential to a modern sports story and often are the best parts of a story.

If your *deadline* for writing the stories is not ridiculously tight, you will probably spend an hour talking to people after the game. The more you've learned about the teams before the game and the more you have paid attention and been focused on your job during the game, the more productive Interview Time will be. Preparation is vital to knowing which questions to ask and to whom to ask them.

Finally, it is time to really start writing.

What's the final tally? At least eight hours of reporting (three during the week, one before the game, three during the game, one after the game) and probably the most time you'll ever get from your editor to write the stories is three hours. That's pretty close to three hours of reporting for every one hour of writing **(See figure 1)**.

While a three-to-one ratio of reporting time-to-writing time is not a rule necessarily taught in journalism courses, it is a practical guideline worth following. Even young writers will routinely follow the three-to-one ratio when it comes to their game stories, as long as they are on deadline. That's because game stories are controlled by time constraints the reporters really have no control over. The game itself will usually take at least three hours, especially when interviewing time is included, and the deadline requirements won't give the reporters much more than an hour's time to write the story.

My experience, both as a writer and as a sports editor working with young writers, indicates that too often the notion of reporting time outweighing writing time is lost when beginning writers are working on a *feature story* and is usually the exact opposite when writing an opinion *column*.

This trap, which I'll call the "over-writing trap," snares every writer from time to time but is one that must be recognized before it can be avoided. If the sportswriter spends an hour staring at a computer screen, struggling to find the perfect phrase or changes a paragraph six times to say basically the same thing, then the sportswriter has been

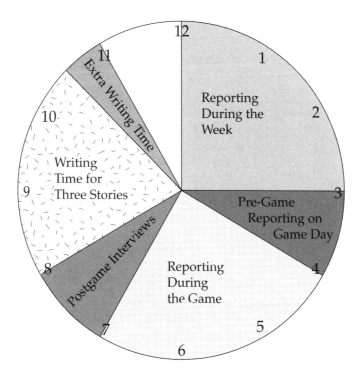

Figure 1: Reporting time vs. writing time. A game-day example.

caught in the over-writing trap. Trying to make the words sing at just the right pitch is a noble effort but it can also be counter-productive and just plain frustrating. What if you had spent some of that time calling another person connected to the story, or doing a little more research? Chances are you will have a more complete story and possibly that key phrase will uncover itself in the course of a conversation.

There are other far less noble reasons for skimping on reporting. It's time to address some of these reasons and explain why they are seldom, if ever, valid.

- **Sportswriters can get lazy.** The reason why a sportswriter might try to get away with the minimal amount of reporting is the same reason a good student might slip up with their studies: Good reporting, like a good research paper, takes time and effort and is a matter of self-discipline. There are days when sportswriters are tired, disorganized or might not be particularly interested in the subject they are covering. They let their negative attitude affect the way they approach their work. Instead of talking to two worthy players, plus the coach, they just talk to the coach after a game. The result? The same as the lazy student: A poor effort translates into a poor grade or, in this case, a sub-par story.

- **Deadline pressure** is another reason that reporting time can be limited. If a game doesn't end until 9 p.m., and your story is due by 10 p.m., then obviously you won't have much time to get comments after the game. In this case, there might be little a sportswriter can do except write the story and send it in as fast as possible. A good reporter, however, will try to get some extra material after the story has been sent. This can be used either for a later edition (most big-city newspapers have more than one edition, with the earliest edition going to the area furthest away from the publication site, and the final edition being for the in-city readers), or for a future story.
- **Sportswriters need to "save hours,"** for later in the week. Unfortunately, this is a reason I heard as sports editor far too often and in fact it had some validity. Working for a relatively small paper, the sportswriters were asked to do a lot of work and it was always implied they should do it in a regular 40-hour work week. In the real world, where extra hours should be paid overtime, it is important for employees to protect their rights and to let management know they intend to be paid for their work. On the other hand, if a story requires some extra hours, the best reporters I've met will put in the time and then worry about overtime pay—not the other way around. These are the writers who recognize that journalism is not a punch-the-clock type of profession. The news and events can and often do dictate your work schedule. You can bet, the game will be played or the local coach will be fired from his job whether you've been cleared for overtime or not.
- **Disliking or feeling intimidated by someone.** These are similar issues that can cause sportswriters (or any journalists) to back away from some extra reporting, though very few will ever willingly admit it's happened to them. Sportswriters and news reporters are often portrayed as tough people who will challenge anyone and could care less what a person thinks of them. The truth is, most reporters do care about other people's opinions and do have feelings. Some would even prefer to avoid a confrontation if they had a choice. What happens, though, is that reporters often have to talk to someone they feel

uncomfortable around, or deal with issues that are painful or uncomfortable for the interview subject to discuss. It's not enjoyable to have to confront a high school athlete about the bad grades that caused him to fail off a team. It's difficult to get through the layers of a college athletic department to get to the heart of a recruiting violation story. It can be uncomfortable to have to write the story about an athlete who has been charged with a crime, especially if you have established a positive rapport with the athlete from past assignments. Difficult or not, reporters who purposely avoid such situations are shirking their reporting duties.

The main reason why sportswriters neglect their reporting duty is not that they are lazy, clock-watching wimps. It is a much more honorable reason. They simply love to write creative stories. Since the story is the end product, there is a tendency to just sit down at the keyboard and begin banging away, hoping that what you just witnessed and the knowledge you already possessed when you sat down and turned on the computer will work well enough.

After all, most people become interested in sports writing in the first place is because they love to watch sports. Then the would-be sportswriters are usually drawn into the profession by the lure of the written word. They enjoy reading good writers and have found that there is pleasure in a well-crafted sentence that conveys just the right meaning.

Alas, very few people are first drawn to sports writing because they enjoy spending hours trying to track down a fact, or attempting to get a comment from someone who doesn't want to speak, and, oh yeah, compiling scoring summaries from 50 or so high school games each night.

Very few would-be sportswriters dream about being cursed at by an angry, aging baseball player who distrusts them immediately just because they have a notebook and pencil in their hand.

That's why it's important to recognize right now that there's more to journalism than just writing. Reporting—the gathering of the information—is the underlining fundamental of all sports writing. It's also what you should be spending two-thirds to three-quarters of your time doing.

Whether it is a straightforward game story, a thought-provoking column or an in-depth feature story, the quality of the reporting done before a sportswriter begins to write the story will be reflected in the finished product. Further, if questions come up during the writing process, then the sportswriter needs to try to find those answers. I do not want to deceive you. Some people are talented enough to write a story that is engaging and entertaining without doing much real reporting. They've seen so much, know so much, and have strong enough opinions that they can get by without doing the real work. But, you know what? That same story could have been better. Anyone who has been in the profession has experienced this. For whatever reason—deadlines, fatigue, lack of interest, or just an honest inability to reach the right person—a question that could have been answered went unanswered. Maybe the average reader doesn't even notice. But the sports reporter/writer knows the story had a hole in it.

The next three chapters of this book will focus on the reporting skills needed to be able to fill the holes in your stories. They will help reveal both the degree of effort that should go into a story and some of the basic tools of the trade that help to get information.

It's important to realize right away that sports writing is just like any other career. It takes hard work to achieve a high level of performance. Young reporters will work long hours. Unless something drastic and wonderful happens to newsroom economics, those long hours will also generate paychecks that are relatively small compared to your buddies who become engineers, lawyers, doctors and computer software geeks. You will almost certainly start at a small-town newspaper writing about small-town athletes. There will be payoffs, however. There will be sunshine and the occasional free hot dog. Most of all, you'll be participating in something that can be different and exciting every single day. Each game has an element of mystery to it, and it's your job to unravel and explain the mystery for the rest of us. Those first years will not be glamorous but they also will seldom be boring. You'll be introduced to sports you may not have even known existed and, if you keep your eyes and ears open, you'll be learning new things every day from an ever-expanding cast of characters.

Be sure to enjoy the moments when it really is a great job. When the excitement of a game is so high that you really can feel the tingle of hairs standing up on your neck and a full stadium of hearty fans are screaming, there are few better places to be. Then there's the adrenaline rush of meeting the deadline and still beating your competitors for that key quote from the star that makes your story the best coverage of the game. Or maybe it's a calmer, peaceful feeling of a cool summer night, watching a baseball game, and enjoying the subtle details of the hit-and-run with peers who share the same passion for the game.

Passion. Perhaps that's the word that best describes why being a sportswriter is a special profession. The sports world is full of people who are intensely interested in their games. Their enthusiasm, combined with your own interests, creates one of those rare environments where people really care about what they are doing because they, like you, have a passion for sports and a passion for people.

Passion for sports. Chances are that if you're reading this book, you already have an intense interest in sports and that's an invaluable commodity. Passion for sports makes the hard and sometimes monotonous work of reporting significantly easier. When a writer learns to transfer their own personal passion into a story with honesty and objectivity it greatly enhances a story.

Passion for people. This may not be something that an aspiring sportswriter has really considered. Do you want to meet new people and get thrust into unfamiliar situations on a daily basis? That's what will happen. You'll learn to stick your hand out for an introduction and raise your voice to ask a question in a press conference. Without people, we don't have much in the way of sports. It is the athletes, coaches, fans, trainers, other media members, team or school administrators who create the games in the first place. They are at the core of the event, and the more you know about them, the better for you as a reporter and thus for the readers at home.

Again we come back to the theme of being a reporter. Get to know the people involved in a game as best you can. It probably won't be the superstars. In today's sports world of huge salaries, off-field endorsements and entourages, the superstars are so restrained and protected by hired assistants that they don't have enough time (not to mention desire) to form anything close to a meaningful relationship with sportswriters. Truth is, almost all athletes and coaches are wary of sportswriters. Some are distrustful of sportswriters. More than a few are openly disdainful of reporters. The best way to tackle the bias against our profession is to be consistently professional. Chances are the athletes and coaches feel they have worked hard at their craft to get where they are. Whether they are major leaguers or Little Leaguers, they know they've put in hours of practice and training. Show these people that you're willing to do the same and, in most cases, you will earn their respect.

It's time to put the keyboard down for a few minutes and start to learn how to be a reporter first, then a sportswriter.

DEFINITIONS:

Reporter: A person who gathers facts, information and descriptions of an event and the people who participated in the event and then writes a story about the event, usually for a newspaper or other media source.

Non-fiction: A type of writing that is based on real-life events, using real names and real people, with stories told in as accurate and truthful a manner as possible. Virtually all sports stories in newspapers are non-fiction.

Deadline: The time when a story, page, section, or entire newspaper must be finished in order to meet the time constraints of getting the paper to the readers. Often times sportswriters have very little time following a game to finish their story, particularly if the game is played at night and the paper is a morning edition.

Game story: A story written about a game or event, usually appearing in the next day's newspaper. The emphasis is on why and how a particular team won or lost the game. Usually the reporter emphasizes the team or teams from within the newspaper's coverage area.

Feature story: A story that gives an in-depth explanation of a particular person, team, or theme that is considered worthy of extra attention. Feature stories are often used to help preview or promote an upcoming event. Usually they are assigned in advance and the writer is given an opportunity to interview not only the main subject of the feature but also several other people who can give insight and opinions that are meaningful. Research is sometimes part of the feature story preparation.

Sidebar story: A combination of the game story and feature, the sidebar is usually written on deadline to supplement a game story but focuses on one particular player or a key play/sequence/decision in the game.

Notebook story: A good place to put all of the little bits of information that are interesting or newsworthy but are not by themselves sufficient for a full story. These are often written to aid in game coverage, serving as a means to update the readers on things like coaching decisions, roster moves, injuries, and pertinent statistics and statistical trends. Notebooks are avidly read by the intense fans.

Column: A story that is purposely written to deliver an opinion or a critique. While the basic rules of good journalism still apply, it is not necessary to state both sides of an issue. Columns are designed to state an opinion, then support that opinion, and to hopefully produce response from the readers.

CHAPTER 2

Fact vs. Fiction

When record-setting slugger Barry Bonds belts a baseball over 500 feet, its majestic arc is like the slope of a great mountain. NBA superstar Michael Jordan soaring to a slam dunk seemed to defy gravity in his early years. Hockey's all-time scoring king, Wayne Gretzky, used to control the puck as if it were metal and his hockey stick was a magnet.

Much in the world of sports borders on fantasy; the great feats of power and speed, the athletes' astronomical salaries, the thousands upon thousands of fans who come out to game after game. Athletes have been written about and given heroes' praise for their skills, stamina and strength for well over 3,000 years. One of the ways the ancient Egyptian pharaohs confirmed their superiority was through great acts of archery and they made sure the public was made aware of the feats by erecting statues with the story inscribed . . . sort of a very ancient—and very permanent—sports section. Homer's great epic works of the Trojan Wars, the *Iliad* and the *Odyssey*, written about 900 BC, are filled with vivid portrayals of games held to honor gods or fallen comrades, with strenuous and exciting contests in running, wrestling, archery, discus and javelin throwing, and chariot racing. Homer's gods and warriors served, at least in a small way, as models for the ancient Olympic athletes of Greece, athletes who would be described, criticized and mythologized by Greek writers for the next 1,000 years.

The connection between great sporting deeds and the desire to write about them seems natural to the human condition. In the past 100 years, though, the connection between sports and the general public has become intensely strong through the combination of sports writing and televised sports. In fact, most of the world could be called "sports crazy," with an almost insatiable desire to learn more and more about the lives and livelihoods of our sports heroes. Whether it's a Brazilian soccer star, an East European weight lifter, a Japanese Sumo wrestler, an Australian swimmer, a Kenyan distance runner, or an American baseball player, athletes have become celebrities, salesmen and—in rarer cases—leaders in their countries.

Throughout the twentieth century the great stars of American sports have been idolized like few other people. The fame of Babe Ruth, Muhammad Ali and Michael Jordan still surpasses that of men and women of their eras who held much more important positions or accomplished things with much greater long-term significance.

Even at the high school level, superior athletes are praised to the point where their status in school is elevated above their peers. They often are given special treatment and certainly receive an undue amount of attention. They are often excused from classes to travel to a sporting event. Those with extra talent are often courted by coaches to play for their teams, sometimes with goodies like free shoes and athletic sportswear used as an enticement. For instance, top high school basketball players are routinely invited to all-star camps around the country to showcase their talents for drooling college coaches. If the players prove themselves superior, then come the scholarship offers, which will include up to five all-expenses paid weekend visits to college campuses. Special? You bet we treat athletes in a special (although not necessarily healthy) way.

Whether you agree with the importance placed on athletic talent or not, let's face the facts. Our country is obsessed with sports.

Athletics, though performed in the realm of reality, has a unique ability to capture and inspire our imagination. This is where the modern sportswriter must be careful. While a sportswriter wants to tap into the creative wonder and excitement that athletes can inspire, a very important part of a sportswriter's job is always to remember that the story needs to stay firmly rooted in reality.

Sports Writing is About Fact, Not Fiction

For all of the wonder and excitement sports can produce, they are still real-life events. Who plays, who scores, and who wins are recorded facts.

A fact is something that has actually happened, or a piece of information or evidence that is recognized—both by the sportswriter and the audience—as being real. Much of the fascination with sports is that so many of the facts *have been recorded.* We can look up how many home runs Hank Aaron hit (755), which country won the 1960 Olympic ice hockey gold medal (the United States), and who the very first winner of the Heisman Trophy was (Jay Berwanger, University of Chicago). With the Internet and a huge array of sports Web sites, now we can find out what Derek Jeter's average is seconds after he singled off Pedro Martinez. These are facts. Facts are the core ingredients of any form of journalism and sports writing is no different.

Fiction, on the other hand, is something invented by the imagination. Some of the best literature ever written is fiction. Chances are your favorite books are fiction. I would encourage you to continue to read fiction. Stretch your imagination and enjoy the wonderful writing of the authors. *Do not, however, start bringing fiction into your sports writing.* Fiction belongs on the bedside table, absolutely not in the newspaper (I'll discuss this more in a minute).

What about opinion? Are sportswriters restricted to only reporting the facts? No. There is a place in sports writing for opinions. Sports columns, which will be the focus of Chapter 10, are by their very nature stories that emphasize the opinion of the sportswriter. Opinions can also be expressed in game stories and feature stories but are usually done through the voices of the players and coaches themselves. In all types of sports writing, opinions should be supported by facts.

What inexperienced sportswriters have to be careful of is making sure fiction doesn't creep into a story. It doesn't usually happen on purpose. The concept of "Don't Make Things Up," is pretty easy to understand. What can happen, however, is that in the effort to use colorful, imaginative language to describe an athlete's extraordinary feat or a team's unbelievable comeback, the description goes too far.

That's when you might start to create something in your story that didn't really happen.

Here's an example:

What actually happened: *The star running back gets free from the grasp of two different tacklers during a 50-yard touchdown run at a crucial time in the game.*

What the sportswriter knows: It was a 50-yard touchdown run. The running back started in the middle of the field and after about 10 yards veered toward the far sideline and then ran to the end zone. He broke at least one tackle in an impressive fashion. The crowd was excited.

The sportswriter is not sure exactly how many tacklers the runner broke away from.

Obviously this was a big play in the game and the sportswriter wants to try to create a sense of excitement in his description. Here are two examples of how the play could be written. Which one do you think is most accurate?

No. 1: With less than five minutes to play in the fourth quarter and the score tied, Johnny Smith brought the home crowd to its feet with a dynamic 50-yard touchdown run. Smith broke one tackle in the clogged middle of the field and at least one more before veering to his left and then outrunning everyone down the sideline.

No. 2: Johnny Smith has a strong sense of dramatic timing. His 50-yard touchdown run with less than five minutes to play and the score tied included a slew of broken tackles and a zigzagging path that covered more ground than a goat on a hillside.

On first read, the second paragraph is probably more fun, and a little more creative. It's also false. First, unless the writer knows that Smith is majoring in the performing arts, he has no idea whether the athlete has any sense of dramatic timing or not. Athletes just play. That first sentence could probably be used if it was re-phrased to read: "Johnny Smith showed a flair for the dramatic," or "It *seemed* Johnny Smith understands dramatic timing." The word "has" says that we know Smith has dramatic timing and that's overstepping our knowledge of the player or the event. More offensive in the second example, however are the phrases, "slew of broken tackles," and "zigzagging path that covered more ground than a goat." A "slew of tackles" certainly sounds like a whole lot more than two. It is misleading. Same with zigzagging path. In fact, Smith only "veered to his left," when he went from the middle of the field to the left side of the field.

Descriptions should be lively and fun when that's appropriate. Just don't forget accuracy. Sportswriters are recording what happened in a game for historical purposes. Don't laugh. Someone will come back to your story in 10, 20, 30 years. They will believe your story to be true, just as we can believe how many homers Hank Aaron hit. It's best to write it that way.

I have heard sportswriters complain that because a game was boring and lacked excitement, their story would also be boring. It doesn't have to be boring, but events cannot be made up or exaggerated in an attempt to add some excitement to a story. That's creating fiction and journalism should never be fiction.

When fiction can represent fact

There is a possible exception to the "no-fiction" rule. Occasionally writers will purposely create a fictional character, usually for use in an opinion column. They make it clear enough to any reader that their friend, or uncle, or matronly neighbor is a make-believe person. Then the sportswriter uses that fictional character to voice a certain opinion, usually in a humorous or instructive manner.

I am not a great fan of such tactics. It's the easy way out when the writer can't find a real person to state the same opinion or the writer wants to distance their own name from the opinion. It can, however, be an effective tool and there have been column writers who have built careers around the advice and opinions of their "uncle Joe." I remember one column I wrote where I had a group of long-dead baseball greats, loosely based on Babe Ruth, Shoeless Joe Jackson, and manager John McGraw, discussing the state of major league baseball. In the spring of 1989, the details of Pete Rose's gambling problem—which would lead to his suspension from baseball that August—were first coming into the national spotlight. Meanwhile, in New England, much was being made of Boston Red Sox third baseman Wade Boggs's extramarital affair. Obviously, I had no idea what Ruth and the rest would say about Rose, Boggs, and baseball in general. It was just a way of trying to put the current situations in the context of baseball history and to point out how changing times have changed the way we expect athletes to behave. In this case, the fictionalized column, reprinted below, gave me plenty of room to voice different opinions before coming to the conclusion that while Rose would remain the all-time hit leader, his gambling would probably keep him out of the Hall of Fame. (It has.) I liked the column and thought it did a good job of putting a different spin on the Rose situation.

One reason it was clear and effective was that the "characters" were obviously dead. They were playing in the Eternal League, after all.

Avoid using such "fictional comments" when the person being "quoted," could actually have been interviewed. In other words, don't make up a column based around fictional quotes from the current star of the local professional baseball team. Since that person is probably routinely quoted in sports stories, it would be easy for a reader to believe your made-up "quotes" to be real.

Troublesome times for the men of the 'Eternal League'
By Steve Craig
Democrat Staff Writer
(March 23, 1989)

In the place where old baseball players go for eternity they discuss the present state of the game and they feel pain. The diamond's luster is fading and the game is taking a beating on morals charges.

For years upon reaching this place the legends of the game pulled on their uniforms, took their cuts, and leaned against bat racks; their youth preserved in an eternal league because the game they had forged still pumped with blood pure.

This spring, though, these men of feats past but not forgotten have begun to stoop. Their swings aren't as crisp, their fastballs have lost a few inches. A sickness has hit them, one and all. The look to the game they left behind and know the root of the malady.

A large man of girth and titanic power, supported by spindly legs, is holding court, as he always does. "I'm awful glad it ain't me getting his life snooped into," he roars. "What that singles-hitting third baseman has himself into is minor league compared to stuff scribes saw me do. But then I was forced out of that town, too."

The Man of Girth draws chuckles as always from his peers. But the laughter is subdued. These men are feeling old, upset by the black marks being rendered by two of the game's brightest stars burning out.

Two huge stars. One, by his record number of hits and incessant hard play, already has a spot reserved among the inner circle of the Eternal League. The other was beginning to merit consideration for a place among the greats, having just moved into a tie for third place in lifetime batting average.

"You know two of the greatest hitters we've seen since we left are having some serious problems," says the man called Shoeless, the man recently tied on the batting list by the singles-hitting third baseman. "And I know what's in store for that Charlie Hustle character if what they say is true." A splat of tobacco juice hits the dugout steps. "I hope it ain't so."

"It doesn't matter if it's so or not," snorts a pudgy, bossy leader that the old players still love. "These guys have been painted bad and there's not enough turpentine to get it off. Them writers write too damn much now."

He knows. He had his share of run-ins with the press. But it never got like this. Even if he was called Little Napoleon with disdain it still had a regal sound. Napoleon scratches the dirt and ponders what it must be like to be called The Chicken Man and begins again.

"You know, big guy, you're right about that third baseman with the Boston nine, he's really just a bush leaguer compared to you but I figure he's going to get his morning coffee in a different city pretty soon."

"And he don't know when to shut up," the Man of Girth adds. "All them TV people actin' like gossip columnists and he just keeps talkin'."

These problems are aging the legends. Their status is linked completely with how their game is regarded and right now they aren't feeling too good. Their bodies creak onto the dugout steps and against the wall they begin to thumb through newspapers looking for some word on a new hard-throwing prospect, or a farmboy slugger, something to brighten the day. Shipped from outposts like New York, Boston and St. Louis (never from Seattle, Toronto, or Oakland), the sports pages offer little solace, though.

"Time has changed so much," Napoleon says. "They still want heroes but they won't let you be human."

These men know what it is to gamble, to womanize, to carouse until the wee hours. They also knew the intricacies of baseball and for them that was enough. They worry that being able to launch a baseball into the stands, executing the daring steal or the swift decision is not enough anymore. Now every athlete has to answer for his actions off the field. Some, like Shoeless, have before but now it seems like everyone does.

> "It's all going to come to a head I fear. Probably before the season starts," Shoeless says. The others understand his pessimism. He knows what it's like to be stripped of privilege and dignity; to be forced from the game. And even though he is accepted by his peers in the Eternal League he still is not allowed into their Grand Hall. At night he must separate himself from the truly great. "The other shoe is about to drop. It might be time."
> "Do they play down there in Florida?" Napoleon asks. "Get all them sportswriters together in one place and all hell will break loose, they'll see to that."
> "Yep, tomorrow in some town called Plant City. The all-time hit leader and a career .356 hitter look like they're going to get ambushed." The Man of Girth has spoken.
> Clouds begin to roll across the skies and in the darkening light the lines on the men's faces lengthen.
> "There could be some rain today," sighs Napoleon.
> "Might not be able to play today," Shoeless notes, adding, "give me a chance to get a bunk ready for Charlie Hustle over with me."
> It's doubtful the rain will come—it never has halted play in the Eternal League. But the Man of Girth stands up and says, "I got a belly ache. Let's not play today." No one disagrees.
> *(Reprinted with permission from Foster's Daily Democrat, Dover, N.H.)*

Unfortunately, fiction does find its way into newspapers and other forms of news reporting in completely inappropriate ways. In 1998, two well-known columnists (not sports columnists) at *The Boston Globe* were alleged to have based some of their columns on information they made up. Patricia Smith was asked to resign. Two months later, Mike Barnicle chose to resign while serving a two-month suspension. Both were (and probably still are) excellent writers who knew what type of stories really impacted their readers. Both also committed what can be called unpardonable sins when it comes to journalism by creating fictional characters for their columns, making up quotes for the fictional characters and—here's the key point—presenting the characters as real people. Smith claimed her make-believe stories accurately represented real events or trends she had witnessed. (Barnicle, who has also been accused of stealing other people's work, simply denied the charges despite large amounts of evidence to the contrary.) The trouble, however, was that both wrote stories that were presented to the readers as real-life, not as fictional accounts used to illustrate issues of concern. There was no way the reader could know that the stories were solely the creation of the writer, complete with dramatic quotes for maximum effect. Both Barnicle and Smith were allegedly doing what is probably the worst thing a journalist can do—they were making up a story.

Here are some rules to live by when it comes to writing any type of news story and they apply to sports stories just as well.

- There's no room for fiction in news reporting of any type. Even opinion columns should be based on factual evidence and first-hand experience. Don't let the fantasy-like aspects of modern-day sports influence your portrayal of a game or the people who play them. They are real people. What they have done is real. Remember, especially as it relates to young athletes, that they also have real feelings.
- Be careful not to overwrite. This is important for any writer. The reason it is relevant to the Fact vs. Fiction theme is that when writers, especially young or inexperienced writers, start getting too fancy they are often prone to exaggeration, which means a reduction in accuracy. The fewer words it takes to get from Point A to Point B, the better. Until you have grown comfortable and confident with the basics, it's also a good idea to avoid multiple ideas or issues if possible. Stick to the main point expressed in the beginning of your story. When you start to weave too many threads into one story, you tend to get fabrication.
- Facts are not dull. They are informative. Just because you can't make things up doesn't mean your stories have to be boring. Usually sporting events have plenty of drama, excitement and suspense. Most athletes—just like most people—have an interesting history to their life. Avoiding fiction does not mean a good sportswriter has to give up creativity and style. Instead, the sportswriter needs to fully utilize the tools of expressive language and to always remember to be a reporter and discover the interesting details or tidbits that can make an impact.
  ◦ Use descriptive adjectives to get across the things you see and hear during an event or an interview: It wasn't just raining, it was an icy, game-long drizzle; the batter didn't just stand at the plate, he scratched his front foot nervously in a half circle while simultaneously tugging the glove on his left hand. Describe the weather, the clothes interview subjects are wearing, the way they arch an eyebrow or clench a jaw.
  ◦ Comments, or what we call quotes, from the athletes and coaches can often give significant insight into an event and

- also tell us something about the character of the individual who is talking.
  ◦ Get details, lots of details, into a story. He's not just a football player. Rather, he is a 6-foot-3, 315-pound defensive tackle who has started 154 consecutive games in the NFL. Now the reader knows the man is big, plays a rugged, physically demanding position and has great durability.
- Avoid generalizations. A generalization is sort of like a prediction, or an expectation. It usually sounds something like this: "Since the 300-pound nose tackle for Wichitummy High School is good, then all 300-pound high school nose tackles are good." Chances are a 300-pound nose tackle, if he's in shape and really wants to play football, is going to be good at the high school level but the statement is wrong and misguided. Have you ever seen really fat kids, who barely fit in their pants, who never get to play? I sure have. They might weigh 300 pounds and I'm sure their parents love 'em, but they are not good football players.

It is easy to slip into a generalization in sports writing, but that doesn't mean you should. It's something to be a little extra diligent to look for in your own writing. Ask yourself, *Can I verify this statement*? Here are a few sample sentences that demonstrate how just a couple of words used slightly differently can change a factual statement into an untrue generalization.

Fact: The Big Ten football conference is stocked with great quarterbacks this year.

Generalization: If you play quarterback in the Big Ten football conference this year you are great.

Fact: Many distance runners admit that they are loners.

Generalization: Distance runners are loners.

In both cases, the generalizations are untrue. The third string QB on the worst team in the Big Ten is not great and just because many distance runners say they are loners doesn't mean we can lump all of them into the "loneliness of the long-distance runner" crowd.

Fiction is dangerous when it comes to a sports or news story. Fiction in a newspaper or a TV news report is like lying to your mother. You know telling Mom a lie is dangerous. Oh, you might get away with it a few times, but sooner or later it's going to get you in trouble. It's the same concept in journalism, only now your lie is being told not only to your mother but to many more people who have put some trust in you as a reporter to get the facts straight and to tell an accurate story. (Remember, both *Boston Globe* columnists did ultimately lose their jobs and their reputations are damaged forever.)

Fiction is also dangerous for another reason called libel. The very word sends shivers of fear up the spine of every editor and it should do the same for every reporter. Libel laws are the public's primary form of protection against reporters or media outlets that stray from the facts or misrepresent the meaning of the facts. If a newspaper is charged with libel in a lawsuit and found guilty, it usually means a very substantial financial loss as well as a significant erosion of the organization's credibility in the community. Even if the media outlet is found innocent, it's still costly. Contesting a libel case is extremely expensive due to legal fees.

The simple fact is this: Report the facts, not fiction.

DEFINITIONS:

Quotes: The exact spoken words of someone interviewed for a newspaper story. They should be framed by quotation marks at the beginning and the end of the statement to let the reader now that these words are from someone other than the author. Quotes should always be attributed, which means the reader must know who made the statement. This is done by simple phrases like, *Smith said, he said, she said,* as in, "I really had the fastball working today," Martinez said.

Libel: The illegal act of using the media to purposely slander (hurt) the reputation of a person or company by the means of misrepresentation of facts, quoting someone incorrectly or by printing inaccurate statements. While there is supposed to be a level of intent to injure for there to be libel, courts are increasingly siding with defendants and any libel case, even if it is won, is costly to a newspaper.

CHAPTER 3

Getting the Facts and Getting Them Straight

Now that you know your sports stories are going to be factually based and not creations of your imagination, it's time to learn how to get enough facts to have a solid story.

That starts with **sources**. The word *sources* will show up with great frequency in this book. Sources are essential for any story. A source is someone or something that provides accurate and representational information for a news or sports story. Usually when sportswriters refer to their "sources," they are talking about the people who have provided information for a story but a source does not have to be a person.

There are three basic categories or types of sources. Sources can be:

- Human
- Reference materials (encyclopedia, dictionary, almanac, media guides)
- Personal observations (the sportswriter's ability to recognize the importance of events)

There are advantages and disadvantages to any source. Human sources have the greatest knowledge and usually have the ability to express that knowledge to someone who is not as well informed. Human sources also have information that only they possess—their personal insights, their memories, even at times their previously withheld secrets. Human sources add interesting insight and depth through their comments, producing the often sought after material that can be used for quotes. The disadvantage of a human source is that humans sometimes aren't as well informed as they think they are. They may tell a sportswriter something is true when they know it isn't, or when they think it is but it turns out not to be.

Reference materials can usually be counted on for accuracy and are certainly not going to lie on purpose. Reference materials, however, can't talk to sportswriters and give them the "inside scoop" on what all the information really means.

Observations are very useful and effective in helping to give the reader a sense of time and place in the story. Simple examples of observations are: *What the weather was like; the condition of a playing field; the look on players' faces as the game wore down; whether the players or coaches were getting angry at officials.* The sportswriter just has to be wary not to turn an observation into an assumption and has to remain as objective as possible when making an observation.

As I emphasized in Chapter One, being a good sportswriter starts with being a good reporter. That means you prepare for an assignment by researching information about the event and making sure you bring the equipment that helps you record what happened: notebook, pen, pencil, tape recorder with tapes, possibly a laptop computer, maybe even a camera. **(see Figure 2).** That means you are observant and concentrating when on assignment. You are also ready to conduct interviews after the game, mostly because the story depends on it but also because you enjoy engaging people in conversation and learning new things. If a key person, say a team's general manager or an injured athlete, happens to be available before the game or during the game, you will try to interview them as well.

Chapter Four will be an in-depth look at interview techniques. For now, we can simply say that **research, concentration and conversation are key ingredients to acquiring the facts.** Research is used when dealing with reference material sources and also human sources. Concentration is important at all times but is vital for being able to make clear and accurate personal observations. Conversation is of course most pivotal when it comes to working with human sources **(see Figure 3).**

To keep the facts straight, however, you need to practice and become proficient with the most basic tool of the reporting trade—note taking.

Getting the Facts and Getting Them Straight 29

Figure 2: A reporter's tools

Taking Notes

It definitely takes practice to be able to hold a reporter's notepad or a legal pad and to write down notes during a game that are both useful and legible. It's even more difficult to do it after a game when you're trying to write down what a coach or player has to say. First, it's important to take notes as the event is happening. Your accuracy is at its best immediately after you have seen something happen, or heard someone say it.

As you're taking notes, think about how the story is shaping up, and whether what you just saw or heard leads you to another question that should be asked.

- In the first half of a girls' basketball game, the coach used all of his players. You make a note to yourself to ask about this substitution strategy. This could be the focus of the story. In the second half, only one reserve player was used. Now you need to change your question, or ask why the second half was different? The vastly different substitution patterns could still be the focus of your story

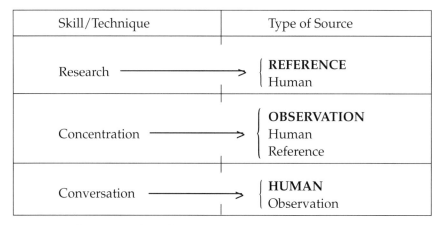

Figure 3: Different skills for different sources. To get the facts, a reporter must use the skills of Research, Concentration and Conversation while working with the three primary types of source information. Sources in bold, all-capital letters indicate the type of source that best matches the reporting technique.

- Jimmy Smith drives in the winning run of a baseball game. You make a note to talk to him. When you begin the conversation, he says that was his first varsity hit. This type of response means Smith is more than an *important* part of the story. Now he is *the story*. You need to ask him, specifically, how much he's played on the varsity, how many at-bats he's had, if he was surprised he was given a chance to hit, and the standards like: How old are you? What grade are you in? How do you spell your name (it could be Smyth or Smitt). Also, go back and ask the coach why he let a kid without a single hit even go up to the plate.

Especially in the second example, one notation taken during the game and then followed up on by the sportswriter leads to a great wealth of new and interesting knowledge. It can also work the other way. Perhaps the sportswriter *is almost positive* Jimmy Smith has never had a varsity hit. Still, since high school teams don't provide reporters with media guides, the sportswriter makes a note to double-check this with the coach and Smith. This time, it turns out that Smith had a hit earlier in the season. The sportswriter might have to re-think how the story will be written (and is probably disappointed that it wasn't Smith's first hit, since that would have "read" better) but most importantly the facts will be accurate.

Game Notes: When I was covering a University of New Hampshire football game as my paper's *beat writer,* I would take notes in two ways. A sportswriter will routinely:

- **Record what happened on the field.** I would keep track of the outcome of each play, noting whether it was a pass or run, who carried or caught the ball, how many yards were gained or lost and, when I thought it was significant, who made the tackle, key block or critical mistake. I tried to make this as complete as possible. This was my record not only to use that day but possibly weeks or even years later. If two years later I wanted to write a story that had a connection to that game, I could go back to my old notes and replay the game on paper (assuming I kept my notes in an easy-to-locate filing system). When covering a high school game, accurate recording of play-by-play results is essential since the sportswriter will in all likelihood have to compile their own statistics. The sportswriter's own "play-by-play" will be his or her only source for both individual and team statistics **(see Figure 4).** Missing just one play can lead to completely flawed statistics.
- **Record what is probably story material.** Not everything that happens in a game is important enough to put into a story (I'll discuss this concept in more detail in Chapter 6). In fact, most of what happens in a game, taken by itself, is insignificant. Think of a 4-yard run in football near midfield, a single cross-court winner in the first set of a Wimbledon tennis match, or one fast-break lay-up in the second quarter of a basketball game. By themselves they are not worth mentioning. Still, you need to record them—in some way—in your notes because they might become part of a pattern: *The football team gets at least 4 yards on every run; by the third set, the tennis player has nailed a dozen cross-court winners; the basketball team is scoring repeatedly on easy fast-break lay-ups.* That's why I would be looking for trends, tendencies, injuries, and other story-shaping elements that required follow-up questions during the post-game interviews. In Figure 4, an example of this is the note that says "Since TD Towson goes" followed by some statistical notes. That note told me that Towson had been stuck with very bad field position four consecutive times. I would then write this and other question-creating notes down somewhere separate from my play-by-play notes, usually on the back cover of

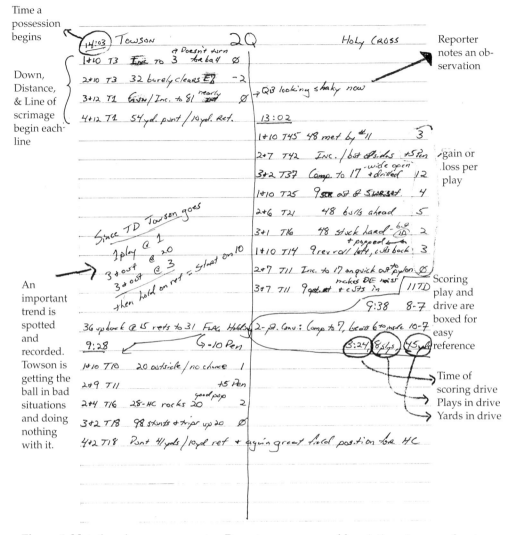

Figure 4: Notations in your own notes. Reporter uses many abbreviations in normal note-taking as can be seen in screened areas. Inc = incomplete; E2 = end zone; Gun = shotgun formation; Int = interception; QB = quarterback; and so on.

the notebook I planned to use during interviews. That way I had a quick reference of questions I wanted to ask, and who I wanted to answer them. I found that this prepared me for the interviews and, in the process, also helped me formulate what the emphasis of my story or stories would be. I would also use simple notations like a star, an underline, or a box to highlight the key plays that I was pretty sure would need to be described.

Post-game notes (a few tips): Especially during an interview, it is very difficult to write down everything that is said and to do it accurately. One thing I noticed over the years was that if I had interviewed a person several times, note taking was easier. You began to hear the rhythm of their speech patterns and could anticipate when they were going to say something that was particularly meaningful. Unfortunately, many people you will interview you've never spoken to—or even met—prior to the interview. This is especially true in a post-game press conference. Some may talk extremely quickly. Others may speak in a whisper. That's why it is OK to use a tape recorder during an interview. There are plenty of varieties on the market that are not that expensive. Look for one that you can easily hold in one hand (along with a notebook), that runs on batteries, and that has good sound quality in its recording. Do not, however, let the tape recorder do all the work. Batteries can wear out. You can drop your tape recorder in a crowd and break it. Wind and other outside noises that human ears can filter out will at times muffle a recorder's clarity. If you are using only your tape recorder and not taking notes at the same time, and for some reason the tape recorder fails, then you lose the interview entirely.

In a one-on-one interview, the reporter should ask the subject first if they feel comfortable being recorded. It is a courtesy, plus, reporters *should not* be trying to deceive someone, or hide their own identity. Leave the hidden recorders to private detectives, the FBI and corrupt politicians. It is your job to let people know who you are, what media outlet you represent, and that you are a professional trying to do the best job you can. Using a tape recorder can help you be more accurate.

Review Your Notes as Soon as Possible

When you're scribbling away frantically, trying to record everything you see and hear, chances are you can't quite keep up. Or, if you're like a lot of reporters (myself included), you may have trouble reading bits of your own writing. Reporters are a lot like doctors and pharmacists. They have horrible penmanship. Maybe it's some subconscious protection method to keep other reporters from being able to sneak a peek at your notes and steal away that one golden nugget you've mined. More likely, it's just that you're writing fast and bringing information into your brain even faster.

A quick review of your notes, while the subject or conversation is still fresh in your mind, will allow you to fill in most of the blanks accurately. By reading one note you took, it will often remind you of something else that is important. This will still happen several hours or even days later but . . . and this is an important *but* . . . unless you are blessed with a photographic memory, the more time that passes, the more detail you will lose from the experience.

It is worth mentioning that learning shorthand would be a wonderful tool for any reporter. Apparently, though, this is simply not taught anymore. I've never seen anyone in the field actually using standard shorthand of the type that every secretary knew 50 years ago. What will happen, and what you should try to do, is to create your own shorthand. Use abbreviations. Write the word "with" as "w/" or "because" as "bcs." Other common abbreviations are "info" for information, a triangle for the word therefore, "btwn" for between. Use initials for the names of people. The baseball box score is home to many wonderful and useful abbreviations: AB (at-bat), HR (home run), 2B (double) and on and on. Learn all of these basic sports abbreviations, often found in the statistical summaries, and make yourself use them. Try to create your personal shorthand when taking notes at a slower pace, such as when you're keeping the play-by-play of a game. In this way, you'll learn to use your own abbreviations and they will gradually become second nature to you. If Larry Bird takes a jumper from the right elbow, or corner, of the free-throw line, then it becomes "33 J RE." The 33 is Bird's number, J stands for jumper and RE is the position on the court. Then the abbreviations will really help you to keep pace when you need to speed your note-

> ### *Be Prepared*
>
> *I worked at a paper in New Hampshire where the weather can be a problem for a reporter who is stuck outside, particularly in winter. Each autumn, our executive editor would put out a memo telling the reporters to be prepared for snow, rain, and cold. Those of us who had seen the memo recycled year after year would chuckle and joke about it: "Oh, it's the 'use a pencil' memo." Why did we call it that? Because the editor would stress how a pencil worked a lot better in a rainstorm or below-freezing temperatures than a pen, and that if you needed to you could "gnaw down to the lead" with your chattering teeth.*
>
> *It definitely sounds funny, but there is an important point: Be prepared. If reporters are cold, soaked to the bone, and don't have anything to write with, chances are they will jump in their cars and go home before they have the whole story. If you're going to be a good reporter, you have to be able to tough it out. It also helps to have rain clothes, pencils and extra notebooks at the ready. A large zip lock bag big enough to cover a clipboard is a good idea, too. When you're going to a game site for the first time, call ahead and find out if they have a pressbox and whether there's room for you.*

taking during an interview. **(Figures 5 and 5a are miniature glossaries of general and baseball-specific abbreviations.)**

The Importance of Being There

The best way to get the facts is to be at an event, especially once a reporter learns what to look for. Whether it's a high school softball game or the spectacle of the Olympics, what is observed first-hand makes a story more accurate and descriptive. Plus, the people you are writing about are usually at the event. This gives the reporter an immediate chance to speak to these people—prime sources for a story—and find out their impact on the game or event and the effect of the game or event on them.

There are times when a sportswriter can get too busy taking notes and will actually miss something that happens during a game. This is another good reason to create some abbreviations, thereby allowing you to note events more quickly. If you find that this is happening frequently during a game, then it is an indication that you are trying to record too much information. While details are very important to a sports story, you also want to be able to properly portray the big picture. My observation is that with experience you will decrease the volume of your notes because you will have a better idea of what is essential to track and what is truly significant and likely to be included in a story. This is a function of experience, though. You almost have to learn how to take too many notes before you can start to learn what is important to be recording and what is insignificant, or can be quickly verified at the end of the game.

The Wonderful Tool Called the Telephone

Every sportswriter should be using the phone on a daily basis. Investment in a wireless phone is probably a good idea for an enterprising young sportswriter. The best way to get facts—especially the facts that really have some bite to them—is by talking to people. These are your human sources. Talk to experts. Talk to the everyday person. Talk to kids, their mothers and their fathers. Reporters may not use all the information they gather, and they may not quote every person they talk to. That doesn't mean the phone call was a waste of time (Well, there will be some that seem like a waste of time because people are poorly informed, are unable to express what they know, or are just plain lying, but even those won't be

Remember, these are suggested as aids to note-taking. **Very few of these abbreviations should ever appear in a finished story.** It would be a mistake to assume the casual sports fan will understand them.

General sports abbreviations
A (assist)
A-A (All-America or all-around)
AAU (Amateur Athletic Union)
ACC (Atlantic Coast Conference;
    Note: Every college athletic conference or professional league has some form of abbreviation. Some leagues are commonly known by their abbreviation, like NFL, NBA and NHL.)
AD (athletic director)
Att (attendance)
Bbl (baseball)
Bkb (basketball)
C (center)
CB (cornerback)
CC (cross country)
Conf (conference)
D (defense or defenseman)
DE (defensive end)
DL (defensive line)
DT (defensive tackle)
EZ (end zone)
FB (fullback)
FG (field goal)
FGA (field goal attempted)
FS (free safety)
FB (football)
FH (field hockey)
FT (free throw)
FTA (free throws attempted)
G (goal, goals, goalie)
GT (goal tending)
HB (halfback)
HC (head coach)
Hoc (hockey)
Ht (height)
HT (halftime)
INT (interception)
J (jump shot in basketball)
K (kicker)
KO (knockout or kickoff)
L (left; often added to a position as in LHB)
LL (Little League)
Lax (lacrosse)
LB (linebacker)
LH (left-hand or left-handed)
LW (left wing)
M (meter or meters, especially useful in track)
NCAA (National Collegiate Athletic Association)
OG (offensive guard)
Opt (option)
OT (offensive tackle)
P (punter)
PA (points against)
PC (penalty corners)
Pct (percentage)
Pen (penalty)
PF (personal fouls; also points-for)
PK (penalty kick; also place-kicker)
QB (quarterback)
R (right, often added to a position like "RHB")
RB (running back)
RH (right-hand or right-hander)
RW (right wing)
S (saves by a goalie; also a safety)
SE (split end)
SOG (shots on goal)
T (technical or technical fouls)
T (tackle)
T (tie)
TD (touchdown)
TE (tight end)
TKO (technical knockout)
Wt (weight)
WB (wing back)
WR (wide receiver)
X-C (also cross-country)
Yd (yard or yards)
3 or 3s (three-point goal in basketball)

Figure 5: Glossary of common sports abbreviations

Getting the Facts and Getting Them Straight 37

> Baseball is full of abbreviations. Many are found in a standard newspaper box score. Some have become part of our common language of baseball, like "W" for a win and especially RBI for "run(s) batted in." Many young sports fans have to figure out the abbreviations before they can understand a box score. The first nine numerals are commonly used not in a box scores but in individual scorebooks by sportswriters, managers, coaches and scorers at all levels.
>
> 1 = pitcher
> 2 = catcher
> 3 = first baseman
> 4 = second baseman
> 5 = third baseman
> 6 = shortstop
> 7 = left fielder
> 8 = center fielder
> 9 = right fielder
> _____
> A (attendance)
> AB (at-bat)
> BA (batting average)
> BI, or RBI (batted in or run batted in)
> C (catcher)
> CF (center field or center fielder)
> DH (designated hitter or doubleheader)
> DP (double play)
> E (error)
> ER (earned runs)
> ERA (earned run average)
> GB (games behind the division or league leader)
> GR2B (ground rule double)
> GW (game-winning as in game-winning hit)
> H (hit)
> HBP (hit-by-pitch)
> HP (home plate, could also be used to refer to the home plate umpire)
> HR (home run)
> IP (innings pitched)
> K (strikeout)
> L (a loss for a pitcher)
> LCF (left-center field)
>
> LD (line drive)
> LF (left field or left fielder)
> LHP (left-handed pitcher)
> LOB (left on base)
> Mgr (manager)
> ML (major leagues or major leaguer)
> MLB (Major League Baseball)
> OF (outfield or outfielder)
> P (pitcher)
> PH (pinch-hit or pinch-hitter)
> PO (putout)
> R (run)
> RCF (right-center field)
> RF (right field or right fielder)
> RHP (right-handed pitcher)
> S (save)
> Sac (sacrifice, usually a bunt)
> SB (stolen base)
> SF (sacrifice fly, which means a run scored)
> SO (another version of strikeout)
> SS (shortstop)
> Sv (another version of save)
> T (time as in time of game)
> TL (Texas Leaguer, a type of high shallow fly ball that just drops in for a hit)
> W (a win for a pitcher)
> WP (wild pitch)
> _____
> 1b (first baseman)
> 1B (single)
> 2b (second baseman)
> 2B (double)
> 3b (third baseman)
> 3B (triple)

Figure 5a: Glossary of baseball abbreviations

a total waste of time. At least you will have learned not to call them again). Almost every conversation adds an additional layer of understanding to the story. When you know more, and understand a subject better, it will be reflected in your story.

The telephone is also a great way to develop more human sources and to stay in touch with the sources you have already established. Sometimes you can also use e-mail to make that initial contact or to keep up to date with a human source. What would be a tremendous habit for a young sportswriter to develop is to get into a regular routine of calling certain sources at certain times on a weekly or bi-weekly basis. Chances are, the source will appreciate the regularity and the fact that you regard him or her as someone important or knowledgeable enough to call every week.

As with so many things in life, there is a caveat, or an exception to the use of the telephone. By its very nature, it hides some aspects of the person being interviewed. You can't see whether a person flinches from a tough question (although a prolonged silence might suggest that), or if a tear wells in one eye, or if a face blushes from embarrassment. Also, people can and do screen their telephone calls either by the use of personal assistants or answering machines and can choose to avoid calling you back. If time and travel allow it, a face-to-face interview is always preferable to a telephone interview.

Use Research Tools

There are a bundle of research tools available to sportswriters, including some that are specifically designed for their use. Here's a listing of some of the common research sources sportswriters can use to get some of the facts and to better prepare themselves for interviews.

- **Media Relations/Sports Information Departments:** Professional teams and most college athletic departments have offices designed to assist journalists with gathering information. They are usually called "media relations" by professional teams and "sports information" departments in the college ranks. This is a valuable time saver for getting details like statistics and background material. One thing to bear in mind, however, is that the media relations/sports information people are publicists for the team. They are supposed to help you but

in the final analysis their loyalties will be with the team, not the reporters. What that means is that when it is necessary to write a story about a controversial aspect of the team (an example would be when a player runs afoul of the law or is suspended from his college team for failing classes), the media relations or sports information person is probably going to be hesitant to tell you everything he or she knows. They may, in fact, have been told to not speak to the media at all on the subject by their bosses.
- **Reference books** are easy to use and are usually quite accurate sources of historical information. There are encyclopedias available which are very complete histories of virtually every person who ever played in the major leagues, NFL, NHL and NBA. They do not offer great insight into how and why an event turned out the way it did but are respected sources for historical references.
- **Past stories:** Your own past stories should be kept in a neat, orderly fashion for future reference. As your career evolves, there will be a couple of star athletes, or particularly successful teams that you will write stories about on a regular basis. It's quite possible, especially if you stay in one region of the country long enough, that you will start writing about an athlete when he is in high school and then follow him through the college ranks and even into professional sports. Believe it or not, those stories about a particular high school triumph might come in handy 10

Truth in the written word?

Many readers of newspapers still believe that if it is in print, it must be true. Well, unfortunately, reporters and editors do make mistakes. Have you ever noticed that even the best papers in the country will run small notices under the heading "Correction"? They do. Every day, hundreds of times across the country.

Don't be fooled into thinking that just because it's on the Internet that it has to be true. Webmasters make mistakes, too, and unless they are diligent and responsive, their mistakes can hang out in the cyberworld for years. Other Web sites are home to extremely radical information. There is very little control of the small, independent site.... No editors, in other words. For that reason, a reporter must be wary of sites marked "unofficial" or that appear to be the rantings and ramblings of a single person. Those sites may offer some insight, but they should not be taken as fact. That's for the reporter to check out.

years down the road when that "kid" is now breaking into the major leagues after four years in college and six years in the minor leagues. Also, beat writers can go over the same topics several times during the course of a single season. Your own stories, commonly called *clips,* can be quick and handy resources if you keep them filed in a manageable, accessible way.

- **The Internet** is crammed with useful tidbits and will someday soon replace the reference book. Plus, it offers different voices, opinions, and slants on the same subject but beware. There is, however, less of a guarantee of accuracy than with published reference books, especially if the Web site is not marked as "official." With unofficial sites it is not always clear what agenda lurks behind the Web site.
- **Other media:** Other newspapers, magazines, and TV reports can often serve as a useful source of background material, especially when used before you conduct an interview. **Warning:** There is something called plagiarism, which means to claim someone else's work as your own. In elementary school it was called copying. PLAGIARISM IS BAD. Reading other reporters' work and learning from them is appropriate. But if you're going to use their words, or a quote they obtained, you *must* give the other media source credit. What you should do with other news sources is to see what they have, let them help point you in a direction, then do your own fact gathering and write your own story. Also, don't assume the other newspaper or TV reporter got the facts straight. Ask those questions or do the research yourself.

Now you understand most of the key fundamentals of reporting, some of which are too often overlooked when it comes to teaching young reporters how to get the facts.

- Sources fall into three major categories: human, reference, observation
- Learn to take notes in a way that is easy and understandable for you.
- Make it a habit to review your notes as promptly as possible.
- Use the information-gathering tools available to you, like the telephone, team publicists, your clips and other media sources, and research guides.

The next stage is putting these fundamentals to their best possible use by learning to be comfortable and confident in an interview situation.

DEFINITIONS

Beat: A specific coverage area or topic. In sports, this usually means a particular team or, if defined more broadly, a particular sport.

Beat writer: A person who is specifically assigned to cover a particular team or sport. Beat writers will almost always write the game story and any previews that are needed. They are expected to react quickly to news within the team or sport.

Clips: A collection of a sportswriter's past stories. Clips are useful for reference and also are used along with a résumé when applying for a job.

Sources: Providers of information for a news or sports story. Usually when sportswriters refer to their sources, they are talking about the people who have provided information for a story. Reference/research guides and books as well as personal observation are also valid sources of information.

CHAPTER 4

The Interview

Interviewing in its most basic sense is having a conversation. The difference is that an interview is not a casual exchange of ideas and comments where people take turns choosing what topics will be discussed. Instead, the interview, by its very nature, puts people into defined roles.

The reporter asks a question; the person being interviewed (known as the interview subject) answers it.

You, as the sportswriter, will listen to the answer. You will be either recording it on a tape recorder or taking notes, preferably both, and doing the best job you can to make an accurate and true record of how the *interview subject* answered the question. Certainly, the aspect of one person taking notes is different from a normal conversation.

The *interview* might at first seem like taking notes in a classroom where the students pay close attention to a teacher and write down the important points of a lesson. The aspects of paying attention and taking notes are similar but the interview is significantly different for one main reason: **The sportswriter has the opportunity to control what's being talked about.**

In many ways, the definition of roles—interviewer and interviewee—takes place from the moment the sportswriter asks an athlete, coach or other potential subject if they have the time to be interviewed. Certainly, as soon as the first question is asked, the "game" of an interview begins as the sportswriter tries to accurately gauge exactly what questions, asked in which manner, will garner the most and the best information.

The second question in the interview might be related to the first answer or it might be a whole new topic. Determining what the next question will be is the job of the sportswriter and is the challenge of conducting an interview. Can the sportswriter get the subject to talk about what the sportswriter needs to know about? Can the sportswriter be quick-thinking enough to change topics when needed? If an answer opens up an area of discussion the sportswriter wasn't prepared for, can the sportswriter adapt and pursue that topic? Is that topic even worth talking about? Is the sportswriter willing to point out to interview subjects that they didn't *really* answer the question but had simply changed the subject? All the questions, though, should be related and connected as much as possible to the specific person the reporter is interviewing.

This means, just as you wouldn't ask a plumber the details of brain surgery, you don't ask a female distance runner questions about basketball, or a football player to explain the differences between a triple axel and a death spiral in figure skating.

The process of question-answer, question-answer continues until either all of the reporter's questions have been answered or, as is more likely to happen, the subject of the interview ends the interview. When it is finished, the reporter hopefully has come away with a much better understanding of the game, the event, or the subject.

The interview is the reporter's best tool when it comes to actually *learning* about a sport, learning the particulars of a game or event, and finding out what motivates athletes and coaches. The sportswriter also gets quotes, which add interesting detail and description to a story, by interviewing people. Interviews explain new information and add to a sportswriter's store of knowledge. Making the interview your best tool takes practice. Appropriate preparation when possible, and a working knowledge of how different interview situations will change the sportswriter's questions and tactics, will end up making the story better.

DIFFERENT TYPES OF INTERVIEWS

The most common types of interview situations will be dealt with in this chapter. Regardless of the type of interview, there is one thing that is generally true: If the sportswriter can engage the interview subject in an easy, conversational tone, it will be an advantage, both in the short term and the long term.

Here's a real-life example. I was fortunate enough to have as part of my responsibility the continued coverage of a world-class female distance runner who lived in our area. Her name is Lynn Jennings, and for a period of about five years she was *the best* female distance runner in the country. A three-time member of the United States Olympic team, Jennings won the World Cross Country Championship three straight years (1990–92), set numerous American records in track and road racing, and won a bronze medal with an American record time at the 1992 Olympics in Barcelona, Spain. We definitely established a rapport. Our roles were always defined as reporter and athlete, but we were able to discuss issues about her career, her past influences and her future goals that she did not share with every reporter. That was the short-term gain. My stories about Jennings were better and more complete than those written about her in any of the New Hampshire newspapers, and they rivaled those done by running magazines. The long-term payoff came following Jennings' bronze medal run when *she called me* from Barcelona only hours after the race. Because of that call, our newspaper had her reaction and insight for our next-day stories. She had also called earlier in the week to let me know how her qualifying run had gone. Like the rest of the New Hampshire media, the paper I worked for did not send a reporter to the Olympics. Jennings did not call any other newspaper. The rest of the sportswriters from New Hampshire had to wait over a week for their home-state heroine to return from Spain before doing interviews.

Certainly, part of the credit for those stories goes to Jennings herself for taking the time to call and recognizing that our newspaper was the most-read media source in the town where she lived. Still, it wouldn't have happened if the sportswriter had not established, through repeated interviews, a level of rapport and respect with the athlete.

As the example of Lynn Jennings and her Olympic call illustrates, interviews can serve a number of purposes, not all of which are directly related to an immediate story. Interviews can take many different forms, often depending on their purpose.

- Interviews are scheduled for the specific purpose of creating one particular story.
- Interviews can be conducted to supplement or add to a story that is planned for the future.
- Interviews can serve as background information for further investigation, which might or might not lead to a story.
- Some interviews are conducted with one sportswriter talking

to one interview subject, face to face, for an extended period of time.
- Other one-to-one interviews may last less than a minute, just long enough for the sportswriter to get the vital piece of information they need.
- Interviews can also take place on the telephone and will range from very brief to very long.
- Occasionally one sportswriter must interview a group of people at the same time.
- It is quite common that several sportswriters will interview one person or a select group of people at the same time.
- Sometimes, as in a professional team's locker room, a whole bunch of reporters are smashed into a small, smelly, loud environment trying to talk to a whole bunch of athletes.

It is important to remember that in each situation the sportswriter should present an image of being a professional who has a job to do and is conducting the interview for that purpose. Any time you are interviewing someone for the first time, be sure to introduce yourself. Look the person in the eye, shake their hand, and tell the interview subject who you are and the **media outlet** you represent. *Hello, my name is Steve Craig. I work for* Foster's Daily Democrat *in Dover. May I talk to you about today's game?* In post-game situations, which tend to be a bit hectic, you might need to do this on more than one occasion with the same coach or athlete until you're sure they recognize who you are and that you have a good reason for needing to speak to them.

The On-the-Spot Interview

The on-the-spot interview is the type reporters will frequently find themselves faced with after a game or an event. The key nature of an on-the-spot interview is that the interview was not planned before the game or event. It is being conducted based upon what has happened or is happening. You may know that you are going to talk to the coach after a game but you choose which players to speak to based on who did what during the game. Therefore, the on-the-spot interview is a type of interview often encountered by someone just starting in the field, since covering a game is usually what beginning sportswriters do the most.

One aspect of the on-the-spot interview is the seemingly simple but often-difficult act of actually finding the person you want to speak with. This is especially true if the game is a high school contest or a college event that has relatively little media coverage. It will be up to the sportswriter to search out the person. At major college or pro events there will usually be someone from the team's media relations department whose job it is to arrange post-game interviews. You will quickly learn which teams do a good job of setting up interviews and which do not. If they don't do a good enough job, then you're back on your own, just as you were when covering a high school game.

Once you've found the person you wish to interview, be sure to introduce yourself and let the person know that you are a reporter and you need to ask them some questions.

Getting the Post-Game Interviews You Need

You can usually be sure a coach will talk to you after a game if you *introduce yourself before the game.* An ideal time to introduce yourself is while the team is going through routine, pre-game drills. This is when the coach is usually just standing on the sidelines, often talking to the other team's coach. It is also a good time to check on a few details: *How did the team do in the last game? Are any players injured? The last time you played this team, what sort of problems did they pose?* Keep the questions short and conversational. Don't become a nuisance. Let them know you would like to speak to them about the game when it is finished.

After any game, it is appropriate to talk to the coach from both teams. This helps bring **objectivity** to your story because you will have the opinions and impressions of both the winning and losing side of the game. To be **objective** is, essentially, to remain neutral or impartial in your reporting. The sportswriter is not *cheering* for one team over the other. Neither should the sportswriter report solely on one team and not explain anything about the opponent. Even when the opponent is from outside the sportswriter's normal coverage area, some description of what type of team they were is important.

While coaches generally know (or quickly learn) to be available to media after a game, the athletes are a little harder to track down. Unless they are professional or major college athletes, chances are they have no idea anyone is going to interview them when the game is finished. There are three basic ways to approach an unsuspecting athlete after a game.

1. Ask the coach to introduce you for the purpose of an interview.
2. Wait for the player to come out of the locker room and introduce yourself.
3. Grab them as soon as the game is over, before they leave the field, and introduce yourself.

The first option is what most coaches would prefer but is not always the best option for the sportswriter. If the coach is cooperative and helps promote interaction between his team and the media, asking the coach first can help create a feeling of trust between the team and the press. The trouble is, all too often the players have already left the field or gym and the coach can't find them. Generally, if the game is indoors (basketball, volleyball, ice hockey) you can be pretty confident that the athletes will change into street clothes and will still be in the building for several minutes after the game. That means you can ask the coach to introduce you. When a high school game is outdoors, players slip away quickly. This is why it's probably best to get their attention as quickly as possible to at least let them know who you are and that you wish to interview them about the game.

Quite often the person you need to interview is someone you have never met before and the questions will be based upon the game or event that has just been completed. First, introduce yourself. Especially with young athletes, tell them why you want to speak to them: *I'd like to ask you about the winning shot . . . I want to talk to you about how it feels to beat your school's arch-rival. . . . I want to ask you about what it was like to guard someone eight inches taller than you.* When it comes to the coaches, usually just saying, *I work for Newspaper X* is sufficient explanation. Respect them if they ask you to wait a couple of minutes. Coaches and players often want to say hello to parents, spouses, girlfriends/boyfriends, or have a quick team meeting before talking to the press.

Use those couple of minutes to your advantage. Before the interview begins, quickly ask yourself three questions.

1. What do I know about this person?
2. What don't I know about this person?
3. What do I need to know about this person? or, to put it slightly differently, What can this person tell me that will help my story?

As you become more experienced, this assessment process will become virtually automatic and you will be doing it before the game is even over.

With this assessment of the future interview subject in mind, jot down a couple of questions that you want to ask and try to tailor them to the specific person. For instance, asking a basketball coach why they chose to play a zone defense in a particular game is a valid question. Asking the same question to the sophomore in his first season on the varsity will usually lead to very little more than an embarrassed "I don't know, 'cause Coach said to, I guess." A newcomer to the varsity isn't going to be wondering *why* a certain defense is being played. He's probably just concerned with whether he even knows how to play it correctly. That type of question puts the inexperienced sophomore in an awkward situation where he is likely to feel uncomfortable. This will result in a poor interview. A better question would be one directly related to his role in the game, something like: *How did you get open for the game-winning shot?* or *Explain why you were playing guard tonight instead of forward as you have in past games?* These questions will lead to answers that will give the reporter an insight into the game that the average fan doesn't have. Also note how the questions are phrased to encourage the interview subject to respond with an explanation or a description, as opposed to a single-word answer.

During the interview, listen

Names, names, names.

The spelling of names has taken an evolutionary path that makes life harder for the sportswriter. With factors like increasing ethnic diversity and a desire for uniqueness, names that sound alike are increasingly spelled in many different ways. It used to be that Amy was spelled A-M-Y and that was that. Not anymore. It could be A-M-Y, A-M-I-E, or A-I-M-E-E. Same goes for the men: Is Brian, B-R-I-A-N, B-R-Y-A-N, or B-R-I-E-N? Possibly you just misheard the name and it's really Bryant or Ryan.

Sometimes people even decide to change the spelling of their names, or their last name changes due to marriage, divorce, or religious choice.

*Here's the point. NEVER ASSUME YOU KNOW HOW TO SPELL SOMEONE'S NAME. Double-check the media guide if there is one. At high school games, ask the scorekeeper **before** the game so you don't forget about it in the excitement of trying to track down interviews. If the scorekeeper gives the slightest hint of not being sure, ask the coach, or better yet, ask the player.*

*In high school sports many of the game results are called in to newspapers by the coaches. One girls' soccer coach I dealt with was extremely diligent, calling each game in, touting his team, and always mentioning his goalie. The goalie had such a long, difficult name that all of the sportswriters on staff always asked how to spell it and the coach always obliged, noting that it was a hyphenated last name. At the end of the season the girl was chosen for our paper's all-star team and came to the office to have her picture taken. By this time I knew how to spell her name, but I asked her to spell it anyway because she was right there. What do you know? Her last name was **not** hyphenated. A small mistake, to be sure, but still a mistake. I am sure the young woman appreciated that I had asked and now it would be correct. The point? Ask people to spell their names.*

carefully to what the athlete/coach is saying (and also what they are not saying). If something they say does not make sense, or if they don't give a very complete answer, then ask them to clarify it. Usually simple phrases like, *I'm sorry, I didn't get that, Which player are you talking about?* or *What do you mean by a 2-3 defense?* will get the interview subject to pause and explain something without sidetracking their thought process too much. Try not to use these interruptive techniques too often as they can become distracting, even irritating.

When a particular on-the-spot interview is done, the reporter should make sure to do at least two more things. First, ask the interview subject to spell their name (see "Names, names, names" section in this chapter). Second, look the interview subject squarely in the eye and thank them for the interview. Increasingly, the sports world has become a land of confrontation that makes the athlete-reporter relationship a mean-spirited *Us vs. Them* situation. Being polite enough to say "thank you" can make you stand out from all the rest of the sportswriters, and it doesn't mean that you can't still be tough when a situation demands it.

On the Lookout for the On-the-Spot Interview

Sometimes an on-the-spot interview will literally stand up right in front of you. It can happen before a game even begins, five minutes after you just sent your story to the editor, or any time in between. Here are a couple of examples of what I'm talking about, both involving owners in professional sports.

As any fan of the New England Patriots can tell you, much of the team's history is tainted by mistakes, misdeeds and misfortune. One such instance was the series of incidents that often goes under the heading of "The Lisa Olson Case." Lisa Olson was a sportswriter for the *Boston Herald* who charged that several of the Patriot players harassed her in the team locker room during the 1990 season. Olson's complaint—taken to Patriots' management—was then reported by *The Boston Globe,* the *Herald*'s arch-rival. Soon the case became an international story with a series of he-said, she-said, they-said, we-reported stories that caused a major explosion of bad publicity for the Patriots and their owner Victor Kiam. It also generated considerable discussion over the rights of female sportswriters to have equal access to locker rooms, as well as the difficulties faced by women sportswriters because they are women. So, when Kiam walked into the press box the next Sunday just a few minutes prior to kickoff, an immediate and impromptu press conference broke out with

Kiam trying to do large amounts of damage control. I worked for a small newspaper that did not regularly cover Patriots games in person. I had made arrangements weeks in advance to come to this particular game to write a story about local athletes who had made it to the NFL. The Lisa Olson saga was not my assigned story. Still, Kiam's pre-game comments, combined with the crowd's increasingly hostile behavior (the Patriots were a horrible team, on their way to a 1-15 season), and Olson's presence while she continued to try to do her job, created a story that simply could not be overlooked—whether I was an out-of-town reporter or not.

The second example was subtle by comparison and involved Bob Bahre, the down-to-earth owner of New Hampshire International Speedway. Bahre and his speedway were responsible for bringing NASCAR Winston Cup auto racing to New Hampshire. The first year the Winston Cup teams came to Bahre's speedway it was quite an event. It was national sports in one of the nation's smallest states. It also could have been a time for Bahre to spend all of his time hanging out with celebrities and big-money corporate executives. Instead, on the day before the big Winston Cup race, shortly after a couple of smaller races had been held, who should be outside the press room window carrying an industrial size black garbage bag and picking up trash? None other than Bob Bahre. It was a moment that required an interview, not so much for what Bahre was going to say but what the moment said about Bahre. Here was the owner of the biggest sporting venue in all of New England, on the eve of the biggest race he had ever promoted, rolling up the sleeves on his trademark white dress shirt picking up garbage. At a time like that, you simply ask the obvious: *Why are you picking up trash?* His answer told a lot about the man. He said it needed to be done and he wanted his racetrack to look nice. Bob Bahre may have made the big time with his sparkling new track but deep down he was still the small-track, hands-on owner who worked harder than any of his employees.

When possible, conduct on-the-spot interviews with just you and the subject. Try to avoid "sharing" the subject with other reporters or with the subjects' friends. You are trying to get information for your story, not someone else's. Nor do you want the subject to be interrupted or distracted by their friends.

The In-Depth, One-on-One Interview

This type of interview is often done for the purpose of writing a feature story. The concept is to get a lot of information from a specific person, quite often to write a story about that person, or someone they are very familiar with.

It is best to set up these interviews in advance, with the sportswriter making a specific appointment. Tell the interview subject why you wish to talk to them. Make sure the time for the meeting is convenient for the subject and allows significant time, usually at least an hour. The reporter's convenience is always secondary, though if your story needs to be finished soon to meet a deadline it doesn't hurt to mention that.

Because this type of interview is pre-arranged, the sportswriter has the great advantage of being able to prepare and to plan a strategy.

- Read as much as possible about the person you are going to interview. This background information can be found in old articles (yours and other writers'), media guides, and increasingly through articles located on the Internet.
- Define in your own mind what you think the story will be about. This probably will involve more than one topic.
- Keep in mind the purpose of the story you will write. Is it going to be a very long feature story on the person you are interviewing? Are you writing something intended to preview The Big Game? Are you introducing a "new star" to your readers?
- Prepare a list of questions based on the purpose of the story. If you are writing a lengthy feature on a well-known star, then your questions need to be designed to bring some new information to the reader, or to address the current status of the big star. If the big star is in the midst of nasty contract negotiations, your questions will be different than if he just won his league's Most Valuable Player award and has already signed a huge contract. If it is a *preview* story, then the questions should be kept relevant to the Big Game. A feature on a new star will require more time spent on gathering background information like where they grew up, their family history, and the stages of their athletic development.
- Decide when certain questions will be asked. Save the tough, controversial, or emotional questions for later in the interview. Hopefully by that time the sportswriter has established some connection to the person they are interviewing.
- Think about how you will react if the interview subject won't answer a certain question. Do you have another question

ready? Do you have knowledge of what they have said in the past on the same topic? If so, ask them if what they said then is still valid.
- Make sure you bring the proper materials for the interview: notepad, more than one writing utensil, tape recorder with batteries and tapes, and a camera in case a unique photo opportunity presents itself.

Also, remember to observe your setting and the subject's reaction to your questions. Are they tense or relaxed? Was it in their home or office? Recording simple facts like this, and then remembering to include them when writing, can make a story more lively and descriptive.

When possible, in-depth, one-on-one interviews should be done in the person's home or at least someplace they choose where they will feel comfortable. Being in someone's home allows the sportswriter to make valuable observations about the person that can bring added detail to the story.

Examples of details you can observe from someone's home:

- Pictures of their children or friends which can lead to personal topics.
- Perhaps some memorabilia from their favorite sports teams.
- The type of home they live in. Is it neat or messy? Large or small? Old or new? In a rough neighborhood or an exclusive suburb?
- Hobbies that they are fond of.
- Do they like a particular type of decorations or furniture?

These details will probably not be the core of the story but they can add great depth. You could just relay the important quotes from the interview but wouldn't the readers know more about the subject if they were told, for instance, that the rising soccer star still lives in his parents' one-story home that includes framed pictures of the rising star from his youth league teams? Through your descriptions of what you, as the sportswriter, have seen, the readers understand that this "star" is still somebody's son who likes to live in the security of his parents' home.

Plus, if a person is willing to invite you into their home, chances are they won't be so quick to try to end the interview.

The Group Interview

Although this situation does not happen frequently, and is best avoided if possible, there are times when a single sportswriter finds they are interviewing three, four, or more people at the same time. This happens frequently when you are writing a story about a particular group of players on a team, like the offensive linemen in football, or the three leading scorers in field hockey, or this year's captains.

The main problem with this story is that you will have a hard time keeping track of who said what. Also, you need to give each person a chance to share his or her opinion. Frequently, one person will answer most of the questions. If it is possible, avoid problems before they arise by asking to speak to each player individually, away from the group. Sometimes, though, the players will not have the time to go through this longer process or they may feel uncomfortable in a one-on-one setting and you will have to start firing away with your questions to the whole group.

Here are some tips for handling this potentially confusing situation.

- Make sure you get everyone's name (with correct spelling), age and/or year in school, and the position they play before asking any of the "real" questions. This is essential because the reporter wants to:
- Ask a question directly to one specific individual. This will allow you to mark on your notepad, usually with the person's initials, who is answering the question.
- Ask them if they are connected in ways outside of the team. Did they grow up together? Do they play alongside each other on other teams? This will help the sportswriter to sort out who the "leader" of the group is and whether the group is also a group away from the field.
- Try to vary your questions. In other words, don't ask the same question to all the people in the group. When you do that, people tend to parrot their friends and give virtually the same response. If they really have a strong opinion that is different from others in the group, frequently they will volunteer it.
- It's always a good idea at the end of the interview to ask if there is anything else the subject wants to add. This is particularly useful in a group interview, since it will allow someone the chance to answer a question someone else was asked and

also afford them the opportunity to sum up what being part of the group means to them.

Imagine this worst-case group interview scenario. The local youth soccer league has just finished building its new, lighted field and will have its first official game that Friday. You call the league president and arrange a meeting at the field on Wednesday. You want a tour of the new field and to find out how it was constructed, how much it cost and how it will be used. Your purpose is to write a story for Friday morning's paper letting the readers know the new soccer field is finished and the first-ever game at the site will be that night.

When you show up for the interview, instead of just the league president, every officer of the league, several coaches, concerned parents and even a few players are on hand. Obviously, all of these people have shown up so they can have their say on a project they are proud of. Now you have a problem. How do you satisfy their desires, conduct a valid interview and not spend the whole night doing something that should have taken less than an hour?

Break the group into small groups for starters. Better yet, ask the sub-groups if they have a representative that can speak for them. That way you end up with one league officer, one parent, one coach and one player. Now you have a manageable group that should offer insight into the project from different perspectives. From this point, follow the general guidelines for a group interview already discussed and remember this key point: **The sportswriter is in control of the interview.** Keep the group talking about the topic that you have come to do a story on. Then, to really show you appreciate everyone's attendance, gather all of them together for a group picture and get everyone's name.

The Pack Interviews

This is basically the reverse of the group interview. Now the reporters outnumber the athlete or coach. There are three basic configurations to media packs and each has some different rules for conduct.

1. **Mob scene:** You have probably seen this situation many times on television—the World Series or Super Bowl star is completely surrounded by reporters with their tape recorders held in outstretched arms. When this situation happens, which is essentially a mob scene, you can just about forget about getting

anything original or unique for your story. Still, you need that quote from the quarterback, so you shove your tape recorder as high as possible and take what you can get.

2. **The Press Conference:** The variation to "mob scene" pack is the more controlled "press conference" pack. These are becoming increasingly common in the sports world. This type of press conference is usually managed by the host team's media relations or sports information director and is very structured. The first thing the sportswriter should do is determine whether this will be the only chance to talk to the coach or athlete prior to the story's deadline. If it is, and you need comments from that person, then hang in there and get the quotes. As always, observe reactions and attitudes. Is the coach/athlete enjoying the spotlight? Are they shy, defensive, excited, controlled, maybe even angry?

3. **The Small or Unguarded Pack:** This is the typical configuration of reporters at a high school event or a smaller college venue. I've also found it's typical of individual sports like auto racing and golf where there are a large number of competitors and sometimes the person who finishes 10th is just as important to talk to as the winner. It also tends to be the norm in locker rooms, where once the star player sits down in front of his locker he's immediately surrounded by a horde of reporters. This type of interview is not organized by anyone. Rather, once one reporter starts talking to a coach or player, the other reporters at the event (sometimes just one or two, sometimes as many as 20 or more) gang up and join in. The real key in this type of interview is to get there first or to outlast everyone else and stay to the end. If you are there first, then you'll have the opportunity to control the interview with *your questions* instead of just listening to the answers to some other reporter's questions.

In these "pack" situations—particularly the mob scene and the press conference—you will probably only have the chance to ask a couple of questions at the most. You need to be specific in what you're asking. Unlike the one-on-one interview, the sportswriter does not have the opportunity or time to ask some easy questions to lead up to the one tough one. That's why press conferences often become confrontational. Each sportswriter is asking their own tough question.

If you feel you have a story or an *angle* on a story that is going to be unique compared to what all the other reporters have, don't give it away with a question in a room full of 100 sportswriters. "Angle" means the particular direction that your story is going to take, or its point of emphasis. On the other hand, listen to their questions to see if they've thought of something that you didn't but should include. Beginning sportswriters can often learn how to ask better questions by listening to those posed by more experienced reporters.

Working in a Pack

Packs can be as small as two or three sportswriters at a high school game or as many as several hundred at major professional events but there are some general guidelines for pack behavior.

1. Ask good, specific questions that will get an answer you need. You may only get one question in. If what you really want to know is why the coach didn't send in his field goal kicker with 57 seconds remaining and his team trailing by two points, then ask, *"Coach, explain why you didn't send in the field goal team with 57 seconds remaining."* If you ask, *"Did you think about kicking a field goal?"* the coach might just say "No," and that's the end of your question.
2. On the other hand, don't ask a question that obviously tips off a unique story or angle to all the other reporters. If you just got a tip that the team is going to make a big trade, don't ask the coach, *"What do you think about the big trade news?"* Save that one for a private one-on-one session.
3. Don't be afraid of breaking away from the pack. That might mean leaving before a press conference is officially over or perhaps never attending it in the first place. If your instincts tell you that you can get more or better information on your own, then go for it.

Clothes Make an Impression

As a group, sportswriters have never been known for their fine clothing. In fact, being rumpled and poorly dressed is a clichéd description of what a sportswriter looks like that, in many cases, is pretty accurate. Still, how you look tells the person you're interviewing something about you. Being clean and presentable is most important. Common sense is also helpful. If you're covering a football game in a rainstorm, your best suit or outfit is not a good idea (see Be Prepared box, Chapter 3). On the opposite end of the spectrum, if you're meeting someone for the first time, cut-off jeans and a tie-dyed shirt isn't your best choice. Be comfortable, be clean and ask yourself, "Would I feel comfortable going to a nice restaurant wearing these clothes?" Hey, if you're a jeans and sneakers person, and a lot of sportswriters are, that will probably work fine.

SUMMARY OF INTERVIEWING KEYS:

There is no single golden rule that will insure a great interview. Instead there are several guidelines that will help you become a better interviewer.

1. Be prepared. Do as much research before an interview as possible.
2. Write down your questions before the interview. Having good, thought-provoking and information-orientated questions ready will make you more confident and thus more at ease. It will also lead to getting information that is actually useful and will usually show the interview subject that you know what you are doing.
3. Be a professional. Don't try to be their best friend or make silly jokes. Avoid asking questions that a sportswriter should already know.
4. Be courteous. Simple things like thanking an interview subject for their time can go a long way, not only during the interview but in future meetings with the same person.
5. Try to create a situation where the interview subject will be cooperative. This may mean setting up the interview in advance or when doing post-game interviews, just letting the coach or athlete have a minute or two to catch their breath and gain their composure after a game.
6. Whenever possible, introduce yourself to a coach before a game and let them know you are there to cover the game and will want to talk to them after the game. This will make your face and purpose known to them when you approach them after an emotional win, and especially after a tough-to-take loss.

7. Whenever possible conduct the interview without other reporters around. This may involve waiting a little bit longer, or leaving a post-game press conference early, but if you think you have a question that will lead to information no one else will have, then it is worth it.
8. Be a good listener. The reporter is not the subject of the interview. Keep your opinions and personal analysis to a minimum.
9. Avoid asking questions that can be answered with one-word, "yes" or "no" responses unless you are specifically looking for a very clear "yes" or "no" response.
10. Unless the interview subject is a well-known athlete or coach, who will likely be offended by such a question, be sure to ask them how to spell their name.

DEFINITIONS:

Interview: The process of asking questions of a person with the purpose of gaining information, either about the person being interviewed, other people, a game, or an event.

Interview subject: The person who is being interviewed by a reporter.

Media outlet: A source of information for the public. Newspapers, magazines, television, radio, and Internet Web sites are the primary media outlets

Angle: The emphasis of a sports story. Usually chosen by the sportswriter in an effort to do one of two things, possibly both: to best represent the most important aspect of a story; or to offer the readers a viewpoint they are not going to find from other media outlets.

Objectivity: When I say a reporter needs to remain "objective" or needs to have "objectivity" when reporting, that means they should strive to report the facts and other elements of the story without personal feeling or personal interpretations.

CHAPTER 5

Writing the Story

Now that you have acquired the needed facts and background knowledge by contacting your human sources, doing research and conducting interviews, you sit down in front of your personal computer or laptop and . . . it dawns on you. "I've done all this work and I still don't have a story."

In the best of situations, the story will almost spring from your fingers right onto the computer screen. That's because all of the reporting work has created a clear understanding of the story. You know what the most important aspect of the story is, who the key individuals in the story are, why the story is important and how the events happened. Plus, you have the background material in the form of statistics, quotes and observations to support every statement as well as the overall theme.

That, however, is the best-case situation. It seldom happens when you begin your career as a sportswriter and doesn't seem to happen often enough even after you've been writing about sports for several years.

For that reason, this chapter will give some basic guidelines for story construction. These are generalizations that can apply to any type of story, whether it's a game story, feature story, opinion column, or even an in-depth investigative series. The main types, or genres, of sports stories will be addressed in the following chapters.

Any sports story can be described as having three primary parts: the lead, the body, and the conclusion.

Lead Off with a Strong Lead

The *lead* (occasionally written as "lede") is the opening statement of the story, usually consisting of between one sentence and three paragraphs. Its purpose is to establish quickly and clearly what the story will be about. The tough part is to do it in an interesting way that will grab the readers' interest enough that they will continue reading the rest of the story.

Many editors and Journalism 101 texts will stress that the lead should answer the time-honored Five Ws of Who, What, Where, When and Why. In theory it makes a lot of sense. The reporter is answering the key questions very quickly. What the editors and beginning journalism studies don't emphasize enough is that Five-W leads are often, in reality, boring, cluttered and sometimes even confusing.

Here's an example of a Five W lead, followed by an alternative lead for the same game:

Five W:
DOVER—The Dover High School boys basketball team defeated rival Spaulding High, 77-68, Tuesday night at Ollie Adams Gym behind 28 points from junior guard Steve Smith.

Alternative:
DOVER—Dover High School junior guard Steve Smith wrote a new chapter of excellence to an old rivalry and brought some excitement to Ollie Adams Gym in the process.

Smith scored 28 points on a variety of jump shots and driving layups as Dover beat neighboring Spaulding, 77-68, Tuesday night.

Neither lead is wrong but the alternative lead immediately lets the reader know that Steve Smith was not only the leading scorer; he will also be the focus of this story. Hopefully the reader will want to know more about how Smith "brought some excitement" into the gym and exactly how he created his offense. For the casual reader who only wanted to know which team won the game, the Five W lead doesn't offer a significant reason to read the rest of the story.

Leads can take many shapes. There should always be clarity and a purpose to the lead. Really good leads compel the readers to find out more about the game, event or subjects.

When you've finished writing the story, go back to the lead and read it again. Look for ways to make it snappier. I once had a copy editor say of one of my leads that I thought was good, "Make it half as long and make it say twice as much." My first reaction was that the copy editor was being rude and not offering any specific help. On further review, though, she was absolutely right. In fewer words, I could give my story a significantly bolder beginning.

Some of you may have heard of the KISS theory (and we're not talking about the '70s rock group with the grotesque makeup and 10-inch platform shoes). KISS stands for Keep It Short and Simple. The KISS theory is always worth remembering when it comes to sports writing or any other type of journalism.

After you've tightened the lead, make sure that your story supports any adjectives or descriptions that you use in the lead. In the alternative lead from above, that means the story must demonstrate *why* Steve Smith's performance was excellent and exciting.

A Strong Body of Information

The *body* of the story is just what the name implies. It is the primary part of the story that will house most of the information you gathered through the reporting process. How big your story's body will grow depends primarily on the space and time allowed for the story. When thinking of the body of a story it might be helpful to compare it to the key parts of the human body—the head, the guts, the arms and legs and a covering of skin that ties it all together. **(Figures 6 and 6a)**

The "head" is the core reason for doing the story in the first place: the explanation to the readers for why this story is important enough to be taking up space on the sports page. Even the simplest game story should have a stated reason for its existence. Too often that reason is only implied, as in *we have a story on last night's Boston Red Sox game because we're a paper located in New England*. A better way is to put the significance of this game into your story.

- The teams' records and league standings and the game's impact on the records and standings can justify the significance of the game.
- As in the example above, the fact that two teams are long-time rivals is enough to justify coverage.
- Attendance figures can be a subtle way to explain why an event was covered, either because many people came to the game or sometimes because no one is coming to watch a team.

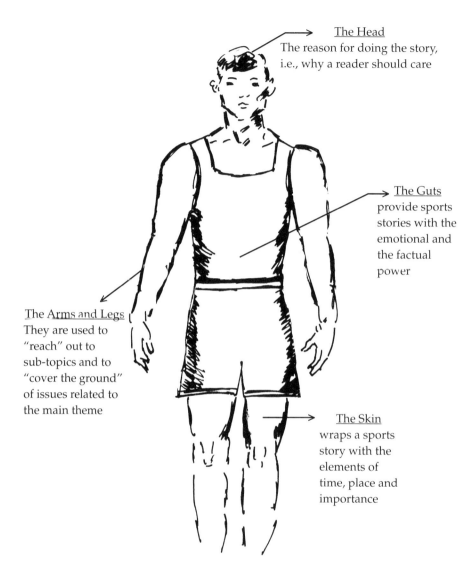

Figure 6: The body of a sports story

In a feature or investigative story the "head" explains to the reader the same thought process the reporter and editors went through: *This gymnast is an interesting story because she is her team's top performer, recently scored a perfect 10.0 in competition but once was so fed up with the sport that she quit as a teenager. . . . We're doing a feature on this college hockey player because he's probably going to be signed to an NHL contract. . . . We're doing a series of stories on the impact of African-Americans in organized sports because it's the*

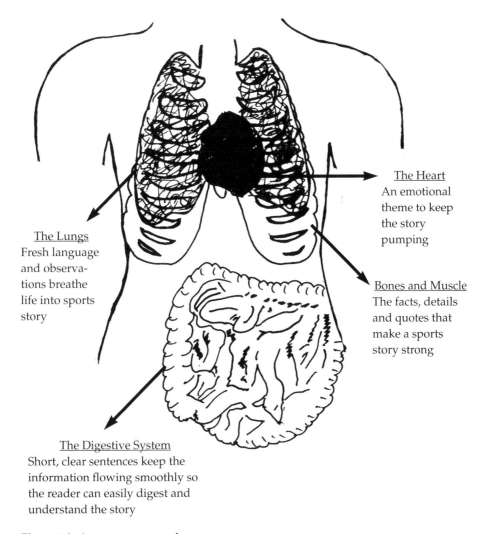

The Heart
An emotional theme to keep the story pumping

The Lungs
Fresh language and observations breathe life into sports story

Bones and Muscle
The facts, details and quotes that make a sports story strong

The Digestive System
Short, clear sentences keep the information flowing smoothly so the reader can easily digest and understand the story

Figure 6A: A sports story needs guts

50th anniversary of Jackie Robinson breaking the color barrier with the Brooklyn Dodgers.

The "guts" of a story covers a wide range of important aspects, not unlike the many facets of your own body's internal organs. There's the heart, or the emotional theme, that keeps the story pumping along. The facts, details and quotes gathered through tireless reporting are like the layers of muscle and bones, adding strength and structure to the story. Good reporters/writers use their choice of descriptive words and the abil-

Datelines

One thing that did not change in the examples of a straight-forward Five W lead and its alternative is that in both cases the first word was "DOVER" written in all upper-case letters. This is called a **dateline** and is a standard part of almost every newspaper story. The dateline is designed to tell the reader where the story took place. There is a potential for confusion, however. Most style books, including The Associated Press Stylebook and Libel Manual, which is the style "bible" in most newsrooms, teach that the dateline should indicate where the **story was written.** Quite often the story is actually written at a location different from where the event takes place. So which spot do you choose for the dateline? The game site or where the sportswriter actually writes the story? It depends on the situation.

Here are some scenarios and explanations that will make dateline choice clearer.

1. The sportswriter is at Fenway Park in Boston and writes the story in the pressbox at Fenway Park. The dateline will always be BOSTON in this case.
2. A game is played in Portsmouth, N.H., but the sportswriter has to make the 20-minute drive back to Dover, N.H., before writing the story. The dateline should be PORTSMOUTH, the site of the game, because a) the game took place in Portsmouth, b) the sportswriter did attend the game in Portsmouth, and c) the vast majority of the information used in the story was gathered in Portsmouth. That the sportswriter was physically sitting in a different town when he or she wrote the story is inconsequential.
3. The game is played in Portsmouth, N.H., but the sportswriter this time works for a different newspaper and drives back to Portland, Maine, before writing the story. In this case the dateline should read: PORTSMOUTH, N.H. Essentially, it's the same scenario as example No. 2, except the reporter crosses a state line. The state abbreviation is added because the event took place outside of the paper's home state (There are a few cities large enough that they never have the state abbreviation included, regardless of which newspaper the story appears in. That's why Boston is always BOSTON, even if the reporter was writing for an out-of-state newspaper. It's best to check the AP stylebook for which cities "stand alone" in a dateline.)
4. The game is played in Nacogdoches, Texas, but the reporter works for a newspaper in Portsmouth, N.H. The reporter hustles enough to get a comment from the coach, via telephone, after the game and then writes a story based on the comment and statistics faxed to the office. The dateline should read PORTSMOUTH, because this is where the story was written. This tells the reader that the reporter was not actually in Texas and did not actually witness the game. I use this example because when I was a sports editor, our paper's primary competitor did just the opposite, putting a "NACOGDOCHES, Texas" dateline on a story when in fact their reporter never left the confines of Portsmouth, N.H. Many small-town newspapers make the mistake (or perhaps do it on purpose) of using a dateline incorrectly. This has the effect of implying that the newspaper is flying its reporters halfway across the country. If the reporter **had** actually been in Texas, then using a NACOGDOCHES, Texas dateline would have been correct.

Some big-city papers skip the dateline when the story takes place in that city, only using datelines when the story originates from an out-of-town location. Beginning sportswriters should always use a dateline with their story, adding the state abbreviation if the story is written from an out-of-state location.

ity to view a story with in-depth insight to breathe fresh perspective into a story, like lungs bringing clean air into our system. What about those nasty intestines? How can we possibly relate a sports story to the human digestive system? Simple. A good story keeps the information flowing smoothly to the reader in clear, understandable sentences. With well-crafted language and logical sequencing the readers can "chew, swallow and digest," a good story. Bad stories create a mental image of "chew it, spit it out," or worse, "I'm not even taking a bite because I can't identify it." Remember the value of KISS (Keep It Short and Simple). If a reader has to stop and ponder exactly what the sportswriter meant by that 35-word explanation in the last paragraph, the reader is probably going to begin searching for the comics.

The hypothetical "arms and legs" are not going to be put to use in every story. These are the sub-topics or related issues to the story's "head" and "heart." While they will create a more pleasing and complete picture of a game or event, they are not necessary for survival. If an editor gives a reporter a limited amount of space and little time to write, then that reporter will have to stick pretty close to the central themes of which team won and why. Some common related issues that would be added if there are time and space would be: how an individual player progressed/regressed; how the win/loss affects the teams' positions in the standings (toward the end of any season this would gain prominence); a comparison to past performances; and a detailed look ahead to the next game or series. The story, like a human, can live without its arms and legs. Using them makes the story more complete. That's why feature stories will almost always be supported by related sub-topics and themes, giving a broader, more in-depth look into the story. Learning to bring the sub-topics and related issues into play even in a brief story will be a sign of clear, concise writing.

The "skin" is that wrapping that puts the story in context in terms of time, place and importance. Oftentimes the outer skin of the story is right in the lead (as in the above example, the reader knows the date and location of the game and that it was a game between rival schools). The human body has several layers of skin. Being able to address the deeper layers that envelop a story comes with experience and the knowledge of the subject gained from some solid reporting.

If you can create a story that has a clear and defined purpose (head), an emotional core that is easy to follow and understand (guts), with plenty of supporting detail (arms and legs) and is wrapped by a consistent theme (skin), then you have the makings of a good story.

Of course, there's always the chance that the **"body"** will become bloated and will suffer from "the curse of verbosity," as former New York *Herald-Tribune* sports editor Stanley Woodward termed it in his 1967 book *Sportswriter*. Verbosity means to talk too much. People who are verbose (politicians come to mind) often lose their audience before they ever get to the point. It's the same with writers. All words should be used carefully. Keep sentences short and clear when possible. Do not make claims that are not supported by facts, comments or personal observations that are contained in the story.

How long is long?

The length of a story is measured in a variety of ways but one thing is constant—they do get measured for length. Different newspapers certainly have different standards. What is considered a short story one day may become "way too long" the next if there is a major, breaking story (long-time coach is fired; star player retires unexpectedly; plane crash kills team members).

So, it is important to learn to write within constraints. That starts by learning how to measure your own stories. Today's computers almost always have a "word count" function and this is very beneficial. Many editors will give their space restrictions in terms of a certain number of words: "Keep it to 500 words," "No more than 1,000 words," or "I'm looking for a real, in-depth piece. You can have 1,500 words."

*A single 8.5x11-inch page of double-spaced type with one-inch margins is roughly 400 words, so 500 words is about a page and a quarter. That translates into the newspaper as approximately 14-16 column inches, depending on the size of the print, the amount of space between each line of print and the standard width of the newspaper's columns (most often two inches). It is my experience that a 500-word game story is an acceptable standard that most editors appreciate as large enough to be thorough but not so big that it clogs the section. (**THE** local team will usually get more space than that.) Most stories in the national newspaper* USA Today *are smaller than that, closer to 350-400 words. You'll notice that there are not a lot of "arms and legs" in* USA Today *stories. They make a central claim, back it up and wrap it up.*

If you find that you are writing game stories in excess of 800 words then, as a general rule, you are overwriting. If an editor asks for 500 words and you hand in 800 words, the story has jumped from a 15-inch space allotment to closer to 24 inches—virtually the equivalent of two tightly written game stories.

In general, preview stories and sidebars are kept in the 500-750 word range (meaning roughly 15-22 column inches or up to two double-spaced typed pages), while feature stories routinely grow to 1,000 words (28-30 column inches, three pages double-spaced) or larger.

Knowing how to convert a story's length from words to column inches to typed pages is a useful trick but not essential for a beginning sportswriter. What is important is learning how the newspaper you are writing for measures its story and then trying your best to write to the length that is requested.

In Conclusion

The *conclusion* is usually a paragraph or two, sometimes as little as a single sentence, that reinforces the thrust of the whole story or, at the least, signals a comprehensible end to the story. In game stories and news stories the conclusion is not as vital, in part because of the **Inverted Pyramid** theory of story construction. This approach, the most common for stories written under tight deadline constraints, puts the most important events in a story right in the beginning, often in the lead, and follows with the rest of the details in descending order of importance. This philosophy can be summed up in practical terms by the first commandment of deadline editing: "Cut from the Bottom." Simply put, if a story is too long and there are only a few minutes left before the printing press is supposed to begin running, the material at the end of the story will be hacked away first. Game stories and breaking news stories are most in danger of falling into this time/space danger zone in the real newspaper world, which is why the inverted pyramid style **(see Figure 7)** is a sportswriter's best choice when writing on deadline.

Still, a conclusion is important. My public speaking professor at Michigan State University, David Ralph, had a mantra for a public speech

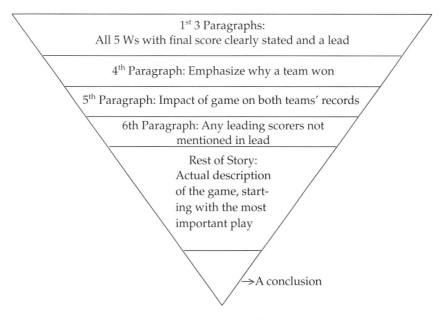

Figure 7: The Inverted Pyramid, or jamming all of the important information in the beginning of a story. A game story example.

that I think fits the printed word concept of lead-body-conclusion just as well. The key to a good speech, Ralph contended, was: "Tell the audience what you're going to tell them, then tell them, then tell them what you told them."

The conclusion acts as a reminder or a summary of what the story was about. When done well, a conclusion leaves a lasting impression the readers will take with them. Good conclusions create emotional responses: tears, laughs, sorrow, empathy, a warm smile, anger.

DEFINITIONS:

Lead (or lede): The opening statement of the story that establishes what the story is about and its context in terms of time, location, and importance.

Body: The primary part of the story that includes most of the information gathered through the reporting process.

Dateline: An all-capitalized notation of the town or city where the story takes place that comes immediately after the reporter's byline and is the first word of a newspaper story. Depending on the circumstances, the state is also included in lower-case type.

Conclusion: The end of the story, usually a paragraph or two, sometimes as little as a single sentence, that reinforces the thrust of the whole story or, at the least, signals an end to the story.

Inverted Pyramid: A common approach to story construction that puts the most important events in a story right in the beginning, often in the lead, and follows with the rest of the details in descending order of importance.

CHAPTER 6

Game Stories

The game story is the foundation of a newspaper's sports section. As the name suggests, it is a story that is a report on a game. It is written for the next edition of the paper, meaning that it appears the day after a game was played if the newspaper is a daily.

The game story is also the story most apt to be skipped or just skimmed over by the average sports fan, especially if it is a major college or professional game. That's because the essential parts of a game story have already been reported by television, radio and Internet services long before a newspaper gets to the reader.

That's one reason that game stories—good game stories—are a challenge to write. The sportswriter has to make sure the key details (like which team won and the final score) are in the story, just like they were on the 11 o'clock news, *and* give the reader some new, interesting information that was not available from the other media outlets.

It's the combination of the essentials and extras that makes newspaper game stories the most complete report on a game of local or national interest.

Let's first look at the parts of a game story that must be included.

The Eight Essential Parts of a Game Story

1. **The final score of the game.** This should be easy to find and near the top of the story. Do not hide it in the final paragraph. It should also be the first score that is given. A good general rule is that the final score should be in the first three paragraphs of a story.

2. **Which teams participated.** Identify the teams by their full name the first time you mention them: the Texas Rangers, the Montreal Canadiens, the University of Connecticut women's basketball team.

3. **Where the game was played.** By this I mean the actual physical location of the game as opposed to just the town or city the game was played in. This would mean the name of the field or stadium should be included

4. **What type of sport was played.** This is often forgotten, overlooked or purposely not included. Generally, when it comes to professional sports it is safe to assume that the reader of a sports section understands what sport they are reading about. When the Boston Red Sox are playing the New York Yankees it is a Major League Baseball game. Not so, however, when it's the University of New Hampshire Wildcats against the University of Vermont Catamounts. In fact, those two universities compete in over a dozen sports.

5. **Identify whether the game is between girls/women or boys/men.** The argument here is much like No. 4. You don't need to say that professional baseball is played by men but you do need to identify whether a high school or college basketball game is a girls'/women's basketball game or a boys'/men's basketball game. (Generally, high school athletes are referred to as boys and girls. They become men and women once in college.)

6. **Identify what league or division the teams are from.** This gives the reader another immediate reference point to help determine what the level of play was. To just say that the game was a baseball game is not enough. It could be a Little League game, a high school game, a minor league game or a men's adult amateur league.

7. **A description of the winning play or the main reason why a team won.** In lower scoring games like soccer, hockey and baseball, usually this means the description of what could be called the winning goal or run needs to be featured prominently. In other sports, like football or basketball, if the game is won in the final moments of play by a particular score, then that would be considered the winning points. If the game is won handily, then you need to describe why one team was significantly superior.

8. **Include both teams' records** and how the outcome affected the league or division standings.

The first seven of the eight essential elements are typically depicted by a late-night television report on your local news channel or cable sports network, either through the use of spoken words, graphics, or the visual highlight material. Often the effect a game has on the teams' records and standings is skipped (particularly on local TV sports reports) due to time constraints.

While it may look like a lot of information, the sportswriter will usually put almost all of it in the first three or four paragraphs of a game story. **See Figure 8 for a story with the Eight Essential Elements highlighted.**

In the example shown in Figure 8, it took just three paragraphs for the story to have all of the essential elements except a clear description of why one team was victorious, though the reason was strongly hinted at with the phrase, *shortened his bench to one sub in the first 38 minutes and the move paid dividends.* A reader could toss the newspaper down right then and know what mattered most about the game. That's good. It shouldn't be difficult for the reader to figure out what happened in a game based upon a sports story. The sportswriter, however, wants the reader to finish the story.

How do you get people to read past the basics? That's the real challenge of a game story.

Making the Game Story Better than Average

Game stories have a tendency to be routine. This is partly because of the eight essential elements. The need to get those key points into every game story and to do it in a quick and clear way makes writing a game story a bit like baking a cake: There is a recipe that is best to follow if you want the finished product to be complete.

Some cakes taste better than others. Game stories, too, can be more appealing if you add some special ingredients—in the right amounts—to your recipe.

Special Ingredients for Game Stories

- Give your game story a snappy lead with some fresh perspective on the event: *UNH continued its mostly fruitless search for*

In the following story, the eight essential elements are in bold.

1. The final score
2. Any teams that played
3. Where the game took place
4. The type of sport that was played
5. Identify whether men or women played
6. Identify the league, conference or division
7. Describe why one team won
8. Include the teams' records

Catamounts club 'Cats
By Steve Craig
Democrat Sports Correspondent

DURHAM—The **University of New Hampshire women's basketball team** continued its mostly fruitless search for success **Friday night** while its opponent appeared to find its elusive answer.

Vermont coach Keith Cieplicki shortened his bench to one sub for the first 38 minutes and the move paid dividends with **a 71-52 victory** before 494 fans at the **sparsely populated Whittemore Center.**

UNH dropped to 6-14 overall and 4-7 in the America East with six conference games remaining on the schedule. It was UNH's third straight loss. The Wildcats will host Hartford Sunday (1 p.m.) at Lundholm Gym. **Vermont improved to 11-8 overall and 7-3 in the league.**

The Catamounts came into Durham with nine players averaging more than 11 minutes per game, eight with more than 20. After a loss to Hartford, Cieplicki decided to "pick a core group and stick with them to give them some confidence. . . . Everyone knew the game plan. It's nice when the game plan works."

Instead of looking tired, **Vermont controlled the rebounding at both ends, forced turnovers and produced excellent offensive shot opportunities all game.** By the time Cieplicki finally sat his six youngsters (one junior, three sophomores and two freshmen make up the sextet), they were ahead 67-43 with 1:59 left in the game. Guard Libby Smith scored 18 and forwards Morgan Hall and Dawn Cressman each had 17. Those three players each had a sequence in the game where they scored at least six straight points.

"I just don't think we gave the type of focused and disciplined effort we needed," UNH coach Sue Johnson said, citing rebounding (Vermont ended with a whopping 53-31 edge) and transition defense as the worst problem areas.

UNH used a more standard rotation of multiple substitutes. The trouble was neither the starters nor the reserves shot the ball well with the exception of sophomore forward Taylore Jarvis (9 points on 4-for-7 shooting). Guard and 3-point specialist Heidi Plencner scored all of her team-high 10 points, six coming in a two-possession stretch with a 27-foot (really!) 3-pointer and then three

Figure 8: The Eight Essential Elements, an example

> free throws when she was fouled on her next trey attempt. The impressive individual effort cut Vermont's lead to 20 with five minutes to play. And that was UNH's highlight.
> "We definitely needed to be a lot more aggressive," said Plencner, a 5-8 junior from Hampton. "As coach put it we just weren't ready to play. We'll definitely be ready Sunday. This is going to be a good learning experience for us. We'll understand we have to be ready right from the start of the game the rest of the season."
> The first half was a recipe for disaster for the UNH women. They committed a bundle of turnovers (11 compared to five for Vermont), were beaten to rebounds and loose balls with alarming regularity and shot poorly (7-of-24 overall, 0-for-6 on 3-point attempts). Vermont's matchup zone defense was able to both sag on the inside options and react quickly to the ball movement to get pressure on UNH's outside shooters. Both Hall, a sophomore out of Hanover High School, and Smith had personal six-point runs. Hall's gave Vermont an early 14-6 edge while Smith's jacked the lead to 22-10. Morgan Brownlee, the only sub in the Vermont rotation, got into the act with a couple of putback baskets that made it 29-15.
> UNH showed some second-half effort to increase its rebounding efficiency in the early minutes and a couple of Anna Mathias inside baskets did trim the lead to 35-24 with 15:41 left in the game. The Wildcats then ran out of answers while Vermont's sizzling six just kept running past them, taking turns doing the damage.
> *(Reprinted with permission from Foster's Daily Democrat, Feb. 3, 2001)*

Figure 8: Continued

> *success Friday night while its opponent appeared to find its elusive answer.*
> - Look for news and when it's there, report it and detail it better than TV or radio can. The news in Figure 8 was that Vermont had drastically changed its substitution pattern.
> - Explain what strategies were used by the teams, how they differed, and why they did or didn't work. This is often hinted or partially explained in the lead, then fully explained in the "body" of the story.
> - Use your post-game interviewing skills to get quotes from the coaches and athletes and then use those quotes in your story as much as allowed by your deadline and the assigned length of the story. Comments from the participants are something TV and radio use only sparingly, if at all.
> - Compare the outcome of the game to a team's past performances and explain how it affects the future of the team. This is easiest to do if the sportswriter has seen the team on a num-

ber of occasions but can also be accomplished by reading past articles about the team and asking the coach and players how they would compare the game to past games. The phrases *6-14 overall and 4-7 in the . . . conference with six conference games remaining* and *third straight loss* are simple explanations of a team's performance over the course of the season.
- Compare individual performances to past efforts as well. Be especially alert for variations or changes, either good or bad, in a player's effort. If a player who is normally a reserve plays twice as much and figures prominently in the outcome, this probably should be the lead of the story. Vermont's decreased substitution was an example of this.

How Do You Describe the Action?

First of all, you will not, nor should you ever, describe every single play that takes place in a game. That would be extremely boring. Your job is to watch the game and decide what is the most important information. In low-scoring games like ice hockey and soccer, you can be pretty sure that each goal should have at least a little bit of description. In football, touchdowns should be included but the more scoring there is in a game, the briefer those descriptions will be. The same goes for baseball. In a 1-0 pitcher's duel, the only run that scores merits some description. In an 11-8 baseball game, that third run scored by the losing team just isn't that important. In a basketball game, you will probably only pick out one or two sequences to highlight, basing your choices on whether the action was crucial to deciding the outcome, was particularly exciting, or both. By sequence I mean a series of plays where something decisive happens, like a team outscoring its opponent 15-0 over a five-minute span.

So how do you decide what to include in your story and, importantly, in what order do you do it? The *most common but not the best approach* is to start with the first score and keep ticking them off, one by one, until you get to the last score. This could be called a chronological game story because it is laid out in order.

A better way of describing the action is based on the Inverted Pyramid method, discussed in Chapter 5. This means the sportswriter decides what is the most important play in the game and puts it first. It may be so important (a game-winning basketball shot from halfcourt as the buzzer sounds) that it needs to be the lead of the story. Or, it might be the best example of your stated reason why a certain team won and therefore would go shortly after the lead. From that point, the sportswriter will take the reader through the other significant details of the game, moving from very important to less important.

The best way of writing a game story doesn't really have a nifty title. The trick here is to continue to back up your overall lead while introducing interesting sub-topics of the game throughout the story. You'll use *statistical evidence* like the game's leading scorers, quotations from coaches and players, and your own observations to give a detailed look at the overall game.

Before the Game

To be able to cover a game, you have to be at the game. That means before you go to an event, a couple of details need to be taken care of. First ask yourself, Where is the game site and how am I going to get there? If you haven't been to a field or stadium before, you better get directions.

Let them know you're coming to the game. Contact the person who oversees the game for the home team and make sure they know you are a sportswriter and you will be attending. This **contact person** is usually the athletic director for a high school game, the sports information director for a college game, and the media relations director at professional events. Tournament games played at neutral sites usually are run by someone from the state or national athletic organization that is sponsoring the tournament, so you may need to contact that organization directly.

Sportswriters who are on the job get to watch games for free. To get that privilege you have to make sure you have the proper *credentials.* Credentials are your verification that you are a sportswriter. Once employed by a newspaper, you will be given a "press pass," which has a picture of you, your name and the name of the newspaper. Certain stadiums, arenas, and events will also issue specific passes, either by mailing them in advance or distributing them "at the gate," which means at the entrance to the game or events. **(Figure 9: Press passes and credentials).** Your press pass and a polite introduction at the ticket gate will usually be all you need for a regular-season high school event, but a pre-game phone call to the host school is a good way of promoting positive relations with the school's athletic department. It's also an opportunity to check on how the team is doing. Often times a high school tournament site will require a special pass which must be requested in advance, usually from the state-wide organization that oversees school sports.

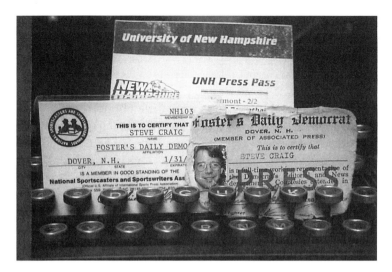

Figure 9: Passes and Credentials. A press pass is helpful and good to have but usually special credentials are needed when attending professional and college games and even some high school events.

Requesting credentials in advance is something that should always be done when covering any college or professional game. At these sites, a sportswriter should never assume their press pass and personal charm is enough to get them into the press box. Plus, since space is often limited in the press box or special press seating, getting credentials in advance will usually reserve you a spot to work during the game.

Once you know that you will be going to a game and you will be admitted, take whatever time you have available to do some reading research, just as you would in preparing for a one-on-one interview. Read about recent games the teams have played. Look for preseason publications or predictions about how the league's coaches or other so-called experts felt a team would do this season. Doing this will familiarize you with the team you are about to see, helping you to identify patterns in their performance worth keeping track of and who the top players are.

The media relations/information departments that support college and professional sports teams will usually produce quite extensive pre-game notes. These will provide the sportswriter with a pile of statistical information and will also alert the sportswriter to newsworthy items like the chance of a record being broken, past records against the opponent, an upcoming or just passed milestone in the coach's career, and the injury status of key performers. These can usually be accessed via the team's Web site, faxed to you, or at the very least picked up the day of the game.

If you are going to be writing your story at the game site (as opposed to at your home or office) you should tell the media relations contact that before the game starts, ideally at the time credentials are requested. They can make sure you have a place to write, a phone line if it is needed, and hopefully an electric outlet to plug in your computer. Or, maybe they will tell you they cannot accommodate your need for a telephone or electric outlet. This happens infrequently but it's a lot better to know about it in advance so you can try to make other arrangements than to find out after the game is over when it will probably be too late.

Get to the game early. There's no worse feeling than knowing you are going to miss the first pitch, the kickoff, or the opening tap. Not only are you going to miss some of the actual game action, but even worse, you are not going to have enough time to properly prepare.

Preparation at the game can take several forms, depending on what type of game you are covering, but there are certain things you always should try to do.

- Get the ***rosters*** of each team and check the spelling of any player's name you are unsure of. Rosters are a list of all the players on a team.
- Find out who is starting the game. For college and pro games, getting the rosters and starters is relatively easy. It's almost always provided for you in the pre-game notes. Not so for a high school contest. It will be up to the sportswriter to go to the scorer's table and copy down the names of the players from the official scorebook. Fortunately, most high school football teams do provide rosters for both teams.
- Introduce yourself to the coaches. Look them in the eye, shake their hands and tell them your name, the name of the newspaper you work for, and that you will want to speak to them once the game is over. Ask a couple of simple questions, like: *Are there any late changes to the starting lineup? Any players missing or hurt for today's game?* Try to do this during routine pre-game drills. Don't interfere with their coaching.
- Get your own reporting tools together. Make sure you have your notebook and your pencils or pens. If you have a laptop computer, make sure it is working properly. If you are going to be sending the game directly to the newspaper's ***copydesk***

from the game site, make sure you know where you will be writing and send a test story to make sure your real story will get where it needs to go.

As you can see, all of these things take some time. If you do not have to write the story at the site and are not worried about plugging in your computer, then you should try to arrive at least 15 minutes early, preferably 30 minutes, to give yourself ample time to get the rosters, introduce yourself to the coaches and get yourself mentally and physically prepared to go to work.

If you will be writing your story on deadline and using a computer, get to the game an hour early. That way you can make sure you have all of the technical stuff taken care of and still give yourself time to get rosters, make introductions and chat with informed people about what is going to happen.

During the Game or "The Art of Tracking a Game"

The main job of a sportswriter during a game is to pay attention and to record what happens by means of taking notes. What I mean by "taking notes" is the way a sportswriter records the action in a play-by-play method that is both easy for the sportswriter to understand and makes it easy to add up the important statistics at the end of the game.

Keeping your own statistics and your own play-by-play is something beginning sportswriters have to learn how to do. My experience tells me that most sportswriters have had to learn this on their own and therefore struggle with taking complete and accurate game notes when they first start.

To be able to keep statistics you need three key things:

- Complete rosters for both teams
- A basic understanding of the sport you are covering
- A system for keeping your notes

For this discussion I will assume you have arrived at the site early enough to get your rosters and already have figured out the basics of the sport you are covering. The job at hand is designing a system for note taking.

Every sportswriter I've witnessed has their own unique methods for taking notes during a game. You will discover your own methods through trial-and-error and practice. Every statistical system, no matter the sport, has some general purposes.

A statistical system should do the following:

- Record the action as it occurs, play-by-play or score-by-score
- Keep track of important individual statistics
- Make it easy to add up or compute the final totals for both the team and individuals

Many sports have specialized *scorebooks* that do an adequate job of recording the play-by-play and a good job of keeping track of when runs, goals or points were scored and who scored them. The best of these scorebooks is undoubtedly the standard baseball scorebook, especially one that is a bit oversized, thus allowing some extra space for specific notes. It is my opinion that any beginning sportswriter should learn how to keep a baseball scorebook in the traditional, standardized manner. See **Figure 10** for an example of a baseball scorebook and an explanation of what the symbols mean.

While many other sport-specific scorebooks are available, the baseball scorebook is the only one I use. The other sports I have covered seem to require a more specialized and individualized style of scorekeeping (at least for a sportswriter) than is allowed by the scorebooks commonly available. A suggestion for a brand-new sportswriter is to ask an experienced sportswriter to demonstrate their technique for scoring a particular sport. The new sportswriter should copy how the veteran sets up their system, then use the veteran's system during a game while watching the game alongside the veteran. Gradually the rookie sportswriter will start to add some new details, delete other things, and eventually it will be the rookie's own system.

Having said that, I will offer my specific systems for basketball, football, and volleyball, along with a very basic, general system that I use for soccer, ice hockey, field hockey and lacrosse. The latter would be easy to adapt to any free-flowing, relatively low-scoring sport. These are not to be taken as the "perfect" examples. Rather they are systems that I use, that work for me, and have been revised and refined over the years. They are not as complete as some statistical nuts might want. What they do offer is a balance between taking notes and still being able to actually watch the game.

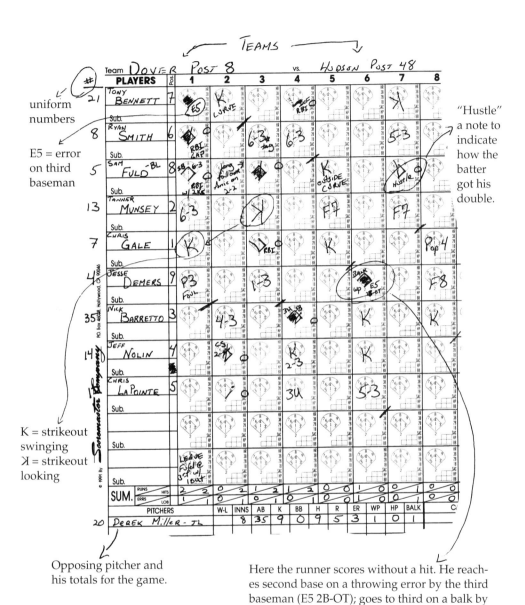

Figure 10: A baseball scorebook

Description of a Basketball Scoring System

I knew I had a good system for covering high school basketball **(see Figure 11)** when one day a college coach of over 20 years was looking over my shoulder while attending one of his son's high school games. "That's great, Stevie. Look at this," he said to one of his colleagues, "the whole game's on one sheet."

Getting to that point in my scorekeeping style was a gradual evolution. For several years I did a play-by-play in a standard 4-inch by 8-inch reporter's notebook, scribbling away and flipping the pages as the game went on. Gradually I added shorthand details like an "x" for a missed shot so I could keep track of a team's shooting percentage. But it was cumbersome to then go back and add up an individual player's points and shooting totals. Under the time constraints of a tight deadline this was a real problem.

What I eventually did was combine the benefits of a scorekeeper's book, which has a line for each player on the team, with the shorthand play-by-play. Instead of the relatively small reporter's notebook, I switched to an 8.5 x 11-inch lined legal pad. That gave me room to write the players' names in the left-hand margin. By drawing in my own lines, I have the individual players' scoring and shot attempts separated into four boxes, one for each quarter. Team shooting is easily figured by adding up all of the makes (2s and 3s) and the misses (Xs) in each quarter. The small vertical lines underneath a team's box are the turnovers in that quarter, something I've found to be an important but under-reported statistic when it comes to high school basketball.

It took a few games to get quick enough to mark down a basket in both the scoring section and the play-by-play section (which takes up the right-hand third of the paper) but the time saved at the end of the game was remarkable since I had each players' scoring totals right in front of me. Plus, I found that I was much more in tune to an individual player's performance during the game. At a glance I could see that a girl who shot 1-for-6 in the first quarter, missing all four of her 3-point attempts, stopped taking the 3s in the second quarter and had shot 4-for-6. Now I could make a judgment that, in this game, the player was more effective when she did not shoot three-pointers.

Of course there are still flaws in my system. I never have been able to chart rebounds effectively. I haven't worried about that much because for me, trying to keep track of one more statistic would detract from my ability to watch the **whole** game. The point is this: Try to keep track of sta-

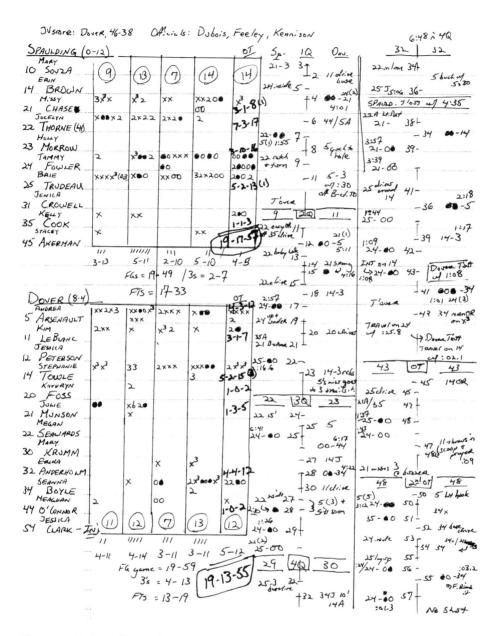

Figure 11: Basketball scoresheet

tistics in a manner that allows for quick and accurate tabulation and adds to your knowledge of what actually happened during the game.

Description of the Football Game Sheet

Much like my basketball method, this was a system I did not immediately use but came to accept as better than my previous method because it helped me add up individual totals much more quickly. The football statistic sheets **(Figure 12)** take a standard approach to charting that I have seen other people use. I like this set-up because of the columns "Run Plyr," "Pass Pssr," and "Pass Rcvr," which allows for easy identification of who ran, pass or caught the ball by use of their jersey number. The "net" column keeps track of the gain or loss for each play. At a glance I can see on the first play of the chart, No. 25 gained 4 yards. Since most high school teams pass the ball infrequently, I've found that I can keep a running total of a quarterback's attempts, completions and yards while the game is going on. It would be relatively easy to do the same for individual rushers, though it is not something I actually do.

There are two obvious but easily worked around flaws in this system. The first is that it doesn't offer a neatly defined area for describing the play. Since there are usually several unused columns on each play, I just jot things down in those. Plus, many plays in a game do not require any extra description beyond what is already noted: the line of scrimmage ("Start Yard" column), the down and distance ("Down"), who carried the ball and how many yards were gained or lost. The second flaw is that the sportswriter has to create some system for making sure he or she knows when the ball has shifted from one team to the other. A trick my sports editor showed me was to use tape to attach the end of a blue pen to the end of a red pen. This way I had a two-tipped, two-colored pen. One team was blue and the other was red. When the possession changed, I just flipped my pen.

At halftime, I add up the individual and team totals from the first half. When the game is over, I add the second half gains and losses on to each player's first-half totals. In this way I have their overall totals as well as a breakdown by half.

Volleyball Score Sheet

Volleyball is a very fast-paced sport. Like virtually every other sport, when it comes to high school competition, you'll have to do your own stat sheet **(Figure 13).**

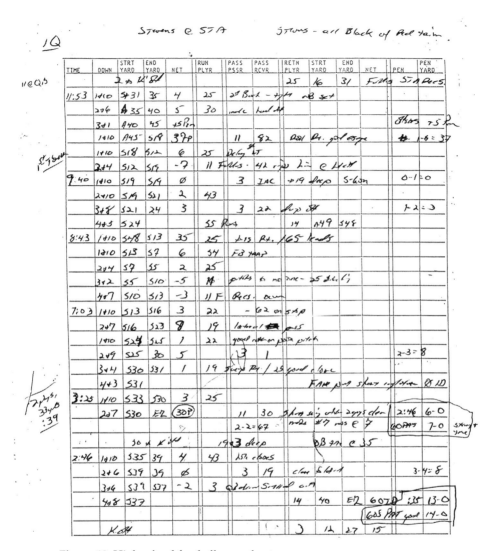

Figure 12: High school football scoresheet

This one is pretty basic but it does keep track of the running score (the middle section of each page), which player is serving (the number in the skinny left- and right-hand columns), and how points and changes of possessions, known as sideouts, were recorded. I use the capital letter "K" to record a "kill," which means any hit that the opposing team is unable to play. So 16K means that the person wearing uniform No. 16 recorded one kill. Missed serves are recorded by symbols "LS" (long serve), "WS"

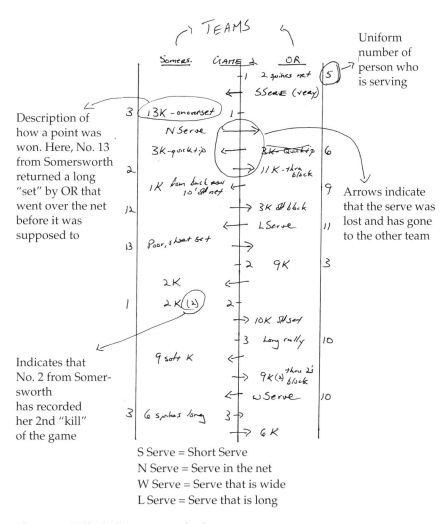

Figure 13: Volleyball scoring method

(wide serve) and "NS" (net serve). A service ace, which means the serve was not played by the opposing team, is written simply as "Ace." While post-match tabulation is slowed a bit because I have to flip through multiple pages of a standard 4 x 8-inch notebook, I do have a record of individual and team totals for kills, serving percentages, and service aces. It also shows me at a glance if any one player had an extended service run, which means their team had a streak of points that is probably worth mentioning in the story.

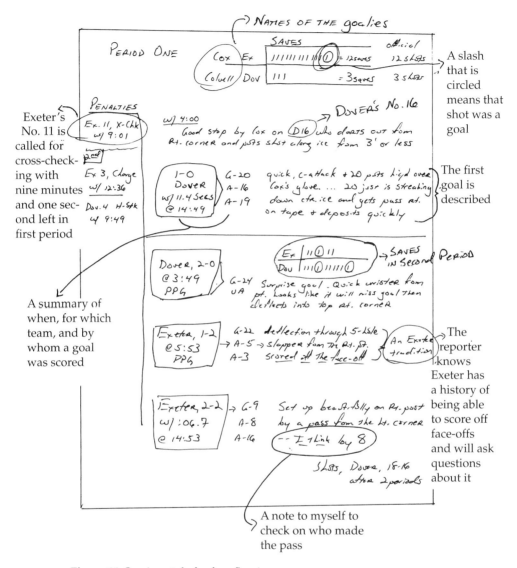

Figure 14: Scoring style for free-flowing games

General Notes for Free-Flowing Games

What I mean by "free-flowing games," are the type of sports that feature numerous changes of possession and action from end-to-end but relatively little scoring. The most common examples of free-flowing games are soccer, ice hockey, field hockey, and lacrosse.

In soccer, field hockey and ice hockey **(Figure 14),** the most important statistic to keep track of other than the actual goal-scorers is the saves made by a goalie. That's done with the simple notation at the top of a legal pad marked "Saves." The reason I keep saves, as opposed to shots, is that shots (shots on goal, at least) can easily be figured out if you have the save

> ## *The roundup, a miniature game story*
>
> *Sportswriters, particularly those at smaller dailies, will be asked to get many short, abbreviated stories on the games that were not covered in person. These are routinely called "roundups," or "summaries." The sportswriter writes the roundup based on information supplied to the newspaper by a representative from the team. Usually this means the sportswriter has had a brief telephone interview with the coach, the assistant coach, or someone the coach has appointed to contact the media. Sometimes the information is faxed to the sports department or posted on a Web site.*
>
> *The form of a roundup differs from paper to paper. Some newspapers get all the information needed for a complete box score from a game, which means every person who played, or at least scored, and then significant team totals. Others write brief one, two or three paragraph descriptions focused on the most important information. Sometimes a "roundup" is stretched because of the importance of the contest or the team involved into nearly a full game story.*
>
> *The standard "box score" or "brief" roundup of games serves as a means of getting all the scores and the major highlights accounted for in each day's paper.*
>
> *Roundups are also excellent training for young sportswriters in the craft of writing quickly, concisely, and asking specific questions to get the "essential elements" of any game story: who played, final score, where was game played, what type of sport was played, boys/men or girls/women, the teams' records, and a description of the key aspect of the game.*
>
> *Taking the example of the previous game story shown in Figure 8, this is how it would be written in roundup style:*
>
>> DURHAM—Using just six players for most of the game, the University of Vermont women's basketball team defeated the University of New Hampshire, 71-52, last night in America East Conference action at the Whittemore Center.
>>
>> UNH, which lost its third straight game, is 6-14 overall and 4-7 in the America East. Vermont (11-8, 7-3) had been using eight players an average of 20 minutes a game before meeting UNH. Vermont led 67-43 with 1:59 left in the game before head coach Keith Cieplicki altered his six-player rotation.
>>
>> The leading scorers for Vermont were Libby Smith with 18 points and Morgan Hall and Dawn Cressman with 17 points each. Heidi Plencner was UNH's leading scorer with 10 points. Vermont had a 53-31 advantage in rebounding.
>>
>> UNH returns to action Sunday, hosting Hartford at Lundholm Gym at 1 p.m.
>
> *You'll note that the third paragraph has information that the game story did not have until much later in the story. That's because leading scorers from both teams and one or two key statistics are commonly mentioned in a roundup. In the game story, the leading scorers were not considered the core reason why Vermont won so they were mentioned later in the story. UNH's next game is mentioned as a service to readers because they are the local team.*

total. It's a simple mathematical formula: Saves + Goals Allowed = Opponent's Shots. If I were doing soccer I would add a column for corner kicks, because they are a good indicator of territorial possession. For field hockey I would add a column for penalty corners, which similarly helps to indicate if a team is controlling the play. (Also, penalty corners and corner kicks can often result in goals or at least good scoring opportunities).

For ice hockey, as this sheet illustrates, I keep track of the penalties assessed in the left-hand margin. Keeping track of penalties is important in ice hockey because the penalized player has to leave the ice for a certain amount of time, resulting in their team having one less skater.

As you can see, the majority of a sheet of paper is left to describe goal-scoring plays or other especially significant events. G-4 means the person wearing uniform number 4 scored the goal. A-7 means the assist went to No. 7 and so on. The time of the goal is recorded as well as the score of the game after the goal. The description part is my personal observation of how the play developed and is essentially a rough draft of what I will write in the actual story.

DEFINITIONS:

Contact person: The representative from a team or organization that will approve press credentials before a game and will be on site at a game to help assist sportswriters and sportscasters.

Credentials: The official approval that allows sportswriters to attend games and events without charge and also gives them access to specially designated areas before, during and after the games that are reserved for members of the media.

Statistical evidence: Also referred to as "statistics," "stats," and "statistical information." These are the numbers that help to define the success and failure of athletes and teams. Batting average, scoring average, points, yards rushing, the splits in a swimming or running event are all statistics. Statistical evidence is a number, or a series of numbers, that supports a claim in a sports story. *Example: Joe Smith is in a batting slump this season.* **He has just one hit in 23 at-bats and has struck out 14 times.** "Smith is in a batting slump" is the statement; "one hit in 23 at-bats" and "struck out 14 times" are the statistical evidence.

Rosters: A list of all the players on a team. Rosters should include at least the first and last names and the uniform number for each player. Rosters will often include other information like position, height and weight, hometown, year in school (or years in the pros), and the high school or college the player attended.

Copydesk: An overall term for the people at a newspaper who are the first to receive and read a story from a sportswriter. Usually, "copy editors" work on the copydesk. When they are done reading the story they will pass it on to the sports editor or page design editor.

Scorebooks: Specialized record-keeping books designed for a specific sport, usually available at general sporting goods retailers.

CHAPTER 7

The Feature Story

     The feature story for the modern sportswriter is like a vast playground for small children. There are so many topics and ideas that can be tackled. Like a child choosing which way they are going to come down a slide or how they will hang from the monkey bars, every feature story can be climbed and conquered with a number of styles and techniques.

     The combination of literally hundreds of feature story ideas (even in a small town) with each having multiple options for how it will be written means the feature story provides plenty of room for the sportswriter to flex his or her creative muscles. Usually these muscles will be toned and strengthened by writing many game stories. The repeated steps of research, reporting, interviewing and actual writing that go into a good game story will help make the young sportswriter strong enough to tackle the exciting concept of feature story writing.

     Game stories and the roundup stories, which I addressed in Chapter 6, are bound by certain rules of construction. Both game stories and their shorter cousins the roundups need to answer the Five Ws (Who, What, When, Where and Why) and they should do it quickly.

     Feature story writing lets the sportswriter use his or her creativity in two major ways: 1. coming up with the story idea in the first place and 2. in the way the story is actually written.

     A good feature story will still answer the Big Five Ws but it doesn't need to be in a hurry to provide those answers. Both the sportswriter and reader have the luxury of not rushing through the process of finding out all the important details. The sportswriter will usually get a little extra time to actually report, research and write the story. The reader will—if the story is done well enough—take the time to enjoy reading the story.

In my opinion, feature stories and well-written columns (which will be addressed in detail in Chapter 10) are the two story styles that will keep people reading their newspaper sports sections in the Internet age. Increasingly, sports news and scores are being retrieved from Web sites moments after a game or event has finished. In fact, there are plenty of sites on the World Wide Web that offer continuous "running" scores and updates of a game that is in progress. Web sites can and do offer the scores for even the most insignificant high school games.

Even without considering the Web's influence, cable television sends televised sports into our homes 24 hours a day, increasingly on more than one channel, complete with scores and news tidbits constantly scrolling across the bottom of the screen. For fans who really need to know what happened to their favorite team in a single game, the newspaper is already yesterday's news. That's why sportswriters have to understand the need to produce better, deeper stories on a daily basis.

Web sites can't satisfy that soothing human need to relax and reflect with a good story while sitting in a favorite easy chair, or on the backyard deck as the morning sun pops over the trees. That's where the full-length, creatively written feature story, complete with appropriate photos and illustrations, still has a strong edge over its Internet competitors. Along with the thought-provoking column and the rare examples of investigative sports journalism, the good feature story is something literally worth wrapping your hands around and holding on to.

TYPES OF FEATURE STORIES

Feature stories can encompass many subjects and approaches. Some of the most common examples of feature stories are:

- **An in-depth portrayal of an individual person.** This generally will provide readers with more information about a familiar athlete or coach or will introduce the reader to a new person who has a significant story.
    - Example A: The star running back of the local college football team is on the verge of breaking the school rushing

record. The sportswriter details why this football player is more successful than anyone else. The sportswriter does this by interviewing the player, his teammates, his coaches and describing the star player's motivations and any difficulties he has overcome.
  - Example B: A 10-year-old girl has begun to show promise as a tennis player despite not being able to walk until she was 6 years old. The sportswriter expands on the theme of overcoming a great adversity by getting as much detail as possible about why she couldn't walk until she was 6 and about the role tennis has played in her life through interviews with the girl, her parents and tennis coaches who have seen her play. The sportswriter makes sure to watch the girl play to judge her abilities and to be able to describe them.

- **A look at the inner workings of a group of people or a team.** This story is designed to explain why the group or team is successful or unsuccessful.
  - Example: A girls' high school soccer team with only two returning varsity players has unexpectedly won its first 10 games of the season. The sportswriter will answer the question of how this group is exceeding expectations, who the key players are, how the two returning players thought the team would do and whether they are surprised by the sudden success. The sportswriter will look for a central approach or theme that defines the character of the team.

- **An explanation of recent trends or innovations in a sport.** These stories have strong elements of news reporting and are sometimes referred to as "enterprise stories." They usually will include some financial references and some overall statistics that show what impact the trend is having on the sport.
  - Example: The local college athletic program has developed men's ice hockey into a national power that plays in front of sold-out crowds. The rest of the college's teams, however, are either unsuccessful or unnoticed, sometimes both. The sportswriter will explain the factors that have led to the one team's rapid rise and detail the shortcomings of the other teams. The sportswriter will talk to coaches, athletes, college administrators and experts from other colleges that have faced similar situations. There will also be a comparison be-

tween men's and women's sports along with an explanation of how resources at the college (money, scholarships, coaching salaries, and practice and game facilities) are distributed among the teams. The theme of the story will be an explanation and a prediction of whether or not some of the other sports can achieve the same level of success as men's ice hockey.

- **A story that previews an upcoming event.** The story could be written with just the basic facts of who is coming, what will happen, where and when the race will be and why the race is held. That would not be considered a "feature preview." Rather it would be more of a simple news notice. A feature preview tries to personalize the event.
    ◦ Example: The lone super speedway in New England is preparing to host one of its annual Winston Cup auto races. The preview will choose a particular hot driver or team to illustrate what can be expected to happen during the weekend's main attraction. The sportswriter will describe why this particular driver is one to watch, through interviews with the driver, his crew chief and his competitors. The key details (The Big Five Ws) about the race weekend will be included in the story.

- **A story about reactions to a past event.**
    ◦ Example A: The local boys' basketball team won its first state championship in 30 years on Saturday. Sunday's paper included coverage of the actual game but because of deadline pressure there was only enough time and staff to have one extra story. Since interest in the team is very high, additional stories are prepared for Monday's paper. Common story ideas might be: the star of the game; the reserve who made unexpected contributions to the winning effort; how the local team's fans reacted to the event; when was the key turning point in the game or the whole season; and a collection of quotes and facts about the game put together in notebook style (see Chapter 9 for more on notebooks).
    ◦ Example B: If the local boys' basketball team is on the verge of winning its first state title in 30 years, then a natural story to develop would be a look back at the last team to accomplish this feat. With this story the sportswriter would interview the players (and coach, if still alive) from that old team,

particularly any that still have a connection to the high school or local community. It's also a good idea to do a phone interview with a former player who has moved out of the area, since their distance from the scene may give them a different perspective and greater willingness to discuss any controversial details. The key to this type of story is presenting the core element of the old team that made them successful, whether it was superior talent, an incredible run of good luck, or excellent teamwork.

- **A first person account of what it is like to participate in a sport or activity,** with the sportswriter's own impressions forming a theme that runs through the story.
    - Example A: The sportswriter steps into a batter's box against a highly regarded high school pitcher and tries to hit the kid's 85-mile-per-hour fastball. The sportswriter uses creative language to tell the readers exactly how fast the fastball seemed, how it felt to be in the situation and in this way uses it as a springboard to tell the young pitcher's story.
    - Example B: The sportswriter knows how to ice skate, but can he or she learn how to do a relatively basic jump that is required in figure skating competitions? The sportswriter would want to supplement their own impressions with comments from area coaches and figure skaters to describe why this elegant athletic endeavor is truly a sport.
    - Example C: The sportswriter takes three laps as a passenger in a race car at well over 150 miles per hour and then tries to drive the car solo. The writer's own description of what 150 miles per hour feels like is central to the story.

    Any first-person story should still include comments and information gathered from interviewing other people, from the real experts to people who are more like the sportswriter in terms of ability level or experience. The reason for trying the sport is to be able to describe the action and specialized details in a way that can only come from participating.

- **An explanation of an unusual sporting event.**
    - Example: A local rugby team is in its second season. Most people have heard of rugby but few people have seen a game in person and even fewer have actually played it. The sportswriter takes an informative and instructive approach, providing a basic summary of rules and unique language.

The sportswriter's own observations of the action and the players' attitudes are an important aspect of the story. Interviews with players and the few spectators in attendance explain both the unique aspects of the game and why it is appealing to the people who play. Unusual sports lend themselves to first-person accounts. Sportswriters need to be aware of their own limitations, however. You don't want the story to end up being how the sportswriter broke his or her leg.

- **A detailed description of one aspect of a game or an event that accompanies the main story on the game or event.** These are usually called sidebars and will be discussed in detail in Chapter 8.

Getting the Idea and Getting to Work

As I already mentioned, there are dozens of good feature ideas all around you. The trick for the sportswriter is to recognize a good feature story idea while doing the other routine aspects of his or her job, like covering games, talking on the phone, and reading other publications.

The best path to good feature stories is paved with sources. What do I mean? It goes back to what I've been trying to stress since the start of the book: **Before you can write, you must report**, and an absolutely essential part of reporting is to develop your sources. Your sources—coaches, knowledgeable parents, players, agents, team insiders like trainers and publicists—will clue you into good feature story ideas. When you take their suggestions and produce top-quality stories, they'll probably give you more suggestions. Plus, they'll remember the professional job you did with their suggestion when you need their help down the road.

The different types of feature stories I mentioned earlier in this chapter should give you some good feature story ideas. When a local team is having its first winning season in several years, that's worth a feature story. When the local area gains a new sports option like a rugby club or an indoor rock climbing facility, that's worth a feature story. You've noticed that all your female friends are playing indoor soccer and several have stopped playing basketball. That's a good indicator that an enterprise story on how soccer is replacing basketball as the most popular game among teenage girls in the area is in order. You've started to take sky-diving lessons so . . . write a first-person account of your first jump.

Here are some tips that can help you to recognize good feature story ideas.

- **Listen to suggestions or comments from readers, editors, team insiders and other reporters.** Sometimes this will be very blatant, as in an editor or a reader saying, "I think you should do a feature story on Jenny White, the volleyball player at Oyster River High School." Chances are if they have thought about it enough to make such a clear suggestion there are some good reasons for finding out more about Jenny White. Other times the suggestion will be subtle ("Does Oyster River have any top volleyball players this year?"). Sometimes it won't even be a suggestion. Rather someone—another reporter or a fan— might ask you for some extra information about a subject ("Do you think Jenny White can get a Division I scholarship?"). When that happens, you should ask yourself, "If they want to know more about this person/team/event, does that mean other people want a more in-depth look at the person/team/event?" If you think the answer is "Yes," then you have a feature story idea.
- **Find story ideas in other newspapers.** This doesn't mean that if your arch-competitor runs a feature story on Jenny White that you have to write one on Jenny White. Instead, look at the theme or the approach of the feature story and then see if it can be applied to your area.
  - Example: A newspaper from the other side of the state did a feature story on an exchange student playing an unfamiliar sport. It detailed the student's adjustment to the new sport and her teammates' adjustment to her. Are there any exchange students in your area that fit that description?
- **Develop features from the news of sports coverage.** A basketball player has consecutive 40-point scoring nights. That's worth a feature on the player. A soccer player is about to score her 100th career goal. Write a feature on her (and maybe do a sidebar on what ever happened to the last local girl who scored 100 career goals). A bowling alley closes after 50 years of business. Write an enterprise story on whether or not bowling is a dying sport and what it means that this one long-standing business has shut its doors for good.

- **Don't always focus on the stars.** Sometimes the best feature stories come from the people who are not in the headlines. My former sports editor came up with a great idea that each spring we would choose six graduating senior athletes to focus full-length feature stories on. We tried to stay away from the star athletes, figuring they had already received plenty of attention by the time they were high school seniors. Instead, we were most concerned about discovering high school athletes who had an interesting story to tell. We did stories on team managers, kids who were better musicians than athletes, players who had to cope with the death of a parent, others who were teenage parents. We did stories on the all-around, straight-A students and on players who struggled with passing their classes. Each year this effort produced six strong stories. Invariably, the best of them were stories that the casual fan and sports section reader would never have known about. How did we learn of them? Primarily through fundamental reporting skills. Sometimes it was remembering a news item from the previous year, or expanding on a topic that had been discussed with the athlete in a previous interview. We also had a brainstorming meeting as a staff. We would think about one school, then break that school into their sports teams, and mention players' names and what we knew about them. Occasionally, when we combined what three sportswriters knew about one athlete, we realized we had a pretty good start to a feature story. Once the series had been established as an annual part of our sports section, we began to get suggestions from readers. Sometimes it was a tip from a coach or athletic director.
- **Look for the unusual, the unique and the overlooked.** What I mean by this is not to look down your nose at a strange sport or a person who seems to be "different." In fact, these will often turn out to be your best stories.
    - Example: In a story I was editing about a local high school basketball game, the reporter at the game mentioned that when the team was awarded a technical foul shot, it sent its team manager, who obviously had a physical handicap, out on the floor to shoot them. This was certainly unusual. To that point, it had been overlooked. In this case I used the "news" from an event and recognized the unique and unusual nature of having a team manager who was obviously "different" shooting technical foul shots. To me, the

situation absolutely cried out, "Feature Story, Feature Story." What was shocking was that our staff was the only one that acted on it and wrote the story, even though the high school team was covered on a regular basis by three daily newspapers and two weeklies. Which brings me to another point. . . .

- **Don't be afraid of the difficult.** The story of the team manager turned technical foul shooter had a facet that made it a delicate story to write. The young man was not just physically handicapped but also was affected by some severe learning disabilities that his parents had a difficult time talking about openly. Obviously this was not a story where the sportswriter could just show up at a game, do a couple of quick interviews, and bang out a story. It had to be planned. The first step was contacting the coach to find out more about the team manager and to get his support for doing the story. That was essential because I needed the coach to help convince the parents to participate in a story that required discussing their son's physical and mental challenges. Also, interviewing the team manager was a bit difficult due to his learning disabilities. Further, there was some question of just how well the other players on the team accepted their team manager. Since the other newspapers were aware of the same basic facts as myself (or at least they should have been), my only guess is that the other sportswriters saw only the obstacles to the story. I'm proud to say that in this instance I saw the value of the story. As it turned out, others agreed. That story won second place in the national Associated Press Sports Editors writing contest for feature stories in the small newspaper category (under 50,000 daily circulation). It is reprinted below.

Earned his shot

By Steve Craig
Democrat Staff Writer

YORK, Maine—For three years the frail boy with the bum right leg, an infectious smile and bad eyesight came to the gym.

He picked up towels and got water for the basketball players. He made trips to high school outposts around the state of Maine. He made friends.

And when the players were practicing at the other end,

he'd quietly take a basketball, position himself at the free throw line and try his luck.

In that way he was like any other team manager dreaming about being one of the guys who wear a uniform instead of picking them up.

But the story of Dennis Phillip Dorey Jr. and how he came to shoot technical foul shots for the York High School basketball team is unlike anyone else's.

One of the first things you notice about Dennis Dorey is his disability.

Dorey was born with cerebral palsy, on Valentine's Day, 1977. It causes him to walk with a prominent limp, swinging his right leg in a half-circle until it's in front of his left. His left foot slides forward and the process is repeated.

"To see him run, you might think he was going to fall over at any point," York head coach Rick Brault explained. "It's a very awkward gait, not question about it. He's just very, very restricted in terms of his movement."

Dorey said matter-of-factly, "Yes, I am handicapped. I wear a brace and I have a bad leg."

Then you realize that Dorey is wearing a York team uniform. Number 11 to be exact. And he's smiling. A smile so big, so pure, it looks as if it could topple the 18-year-old senior over.

Because of his physical challenges, Dorey cannot play basketball. But he can ... and does ... contribute. While the game swirls in front of him, Dorey waits for his opportunity.

His role is definite. He shoots technical foul shots.

All of them. No matter where, no matter when.

"He has shown tremendous loyalty. He's been around the program so long. This is a role that he deserves ... and one he has earned," Brault said.

Dorey's association with York basketball began his freshman year shortly after his parents Faye and Dennis Sr., moved from Portsmouth to a home they had built in Cape Neddick.

"One of our primary concerns as a staff was we wanted to get him socially connected to the school," Brault said.

Brault took Dorey on as a team manager.

"I don't know if he fell in love with the game but he certainly took a liking to the game of basketball," Brault said. "He started picking up the basketball and throwing it around and at the foul line he'd almost make it. Then he'd occasionally throw one in and we'd give him encouragement to keep trying."

One day during Dorey's junior year, Brault approached him with an idea.

"I said if you can make seven of 10 we'll hold a jersey for you. Do that and you'll dress with the team for games, become a player-manager and be our technical foul shooter," Brault said.

"He worked hard enough to do it and this is just a follow-through on a promise made," Brault said.

There will be no exceptions. If York is playing for the state title, with the game on the line in the final minute and a technical is called, Dorey will shoot it.

"That's a decision I made and a decision the team made," Brault said. "If there's any people in the stands that are going to question that decision then I don't want to hear it."

It is legal for a coach to sub a technical foul shooter. It's just not done very often.

Imagine a coach calling on the last player on the bench to go out in front of a big crowd, with all eyes trained on him, and shoot a free throw without any warmup. The coach would be run out of town.

Now imagine that player wearing a plastic brace on his leg, limping to the stripe and lining up an under-handed attempt.

That's exactly what Brault has done this season. Instead of jeers, the move has brought nothing but cheers. Instead of panicking, Dorey has anxiously awaited each opportunity to be center stage.

"No, I wasn't scared at all," Dorey said. "It makes me feel pretty happy in that they're all cheering for me."

Dorey has made two of his eight attempts.

"Wouldn't you say that's respectable, coming off the bench with the crowd hooting and hollering?" Brault asked.

Dorey's first varsity point came last Dec. 15, against arch-rival Marshwood. There was 2:34 to play in the game with

York holding a precarious one-point lead when the technical was called and the buzz began.

Dorey calmly drained the free throw.

"When he made that shot the whole bleachers shook," Dennis Dorey Sr. remembered. "The whole building shook. Geez, it sure seemed like it. Even the other team's fans were rooting for him."

"It felt pretty good. I just knew that the shot was there and it was going to go in," Dorey recalled. "I felt pretty good about it and the team was happy for me that I hit the shot."

The acceptance of his teammates and the crowd has been pivotal in making Dorey's story a success.

"The crowd could have ruined everything. And the players could have, too," Dorey's father said. "But that didn't happen. They players have been real good to him and the crowd has, too."

In turn, Dorey has given something to his team much greater than two points.

"I look up to Dennis, really," senior Zack Huntsman said. "You have to appreciate the effort of him coming out here and doing what he's done."

"It goes right back to the people," Dennis Dorey Sr. said. "If you're wanted, it makes it good for you. But if you're not wanted it wouldn't make it too enjoyable, would it?"

There's little doubt that Dorey, who is on line to graduate in the spring with his senior class, is appreciated by his teammates. The genuine affection Brault feels for the young man is obvious.

"He's an inspiration," Brault said. "You take a look at Dennis and his handicaps, and then you look at yourself and you can't help but be inspired by how much he's overcome."

(Reprinted with permission from Foster's Daily Democrat, Dover, N.H., Feb. 2, 1996)

A Preparation Strategy for Feature Stories

Feature stories require more time and effort than a game story if they are going to be the type of well-crafted, effective story that really involves the reader. Since most editors recognize this, you will usually be given some extra time to both report and write a feature story. Still, you want to use that extra time wisely and effectively. Following these general guidelines should ease the reporting effort and also will serve you well when it comes time to actually write the story.

1. **Define your story idea.** This might be as simple as, *I want to do a story on Dover High's star baseball player because he's a great high school hitter,* or as complex as, *With the star of Dover High's baseball team as my main subject, I want to write a story that will detail the scientific properties of what happens when a wooden bat meets a hard ball wrapped in rawhide.*

2. **Figure out what you need to research.** If the point of the story is the player, then you need to find out the Dover High star's hitting statistics over the previous three seasons. If you're going with the sports-meets-science story, then you better start learning about the scientific theories concerning mass, inertia and atmospheric resistance.

3. **Make a rough outline of the story.** Let's say you've decided to scrap the physics theory (good choice) and will focus on the baseball player. A rough outline could go something like this:

    a. A brief description of how powerful a hitter this kid is.

    b. The star player's hopes for the rest of the season and his future goals.

    c. Comments from coach and teammates that back up the claim that the kid is a great hitter.

    d. Discussion of his family background. Explain how his family has been supportive; perhaps there have been difficulties (divorce, death of a parent) the athlete has had to overcome. Explain the character and mental makeup of the player.

    e. A conclusion that sums up the kid's past and his promise.

4. **What are the key questions that need to be answered?** In this case, you need to find out the star hitter's batting statistics, what his future goals are, whether he can realistically achieve any or all of them, what factors have led him to becoming such a good hitter, and the influence his family and background have had on him.

5. **Figure out who needs to be interviewed.** This should be done with the dual purpose of getting the answers to the questions you know you want to ask and also talking to people who can tell you more about the star athlete than you already know or suspect. It's often quite helpful to interview the person who is the focus of the story *after* you have interviewed other people, like his coach or teammates, who can offer insight into the athlete's personality and approach to the sport. Whenever doing

a feature story on a high school athlete, it's worth the time to talk to his or her parents.

6. **Conduct your interviews.**

WRITING THE FEATURE STORY

Whether the focus of the feature story is an individual or an entire athletic department, great feature stories need to:

- **Create a mood.** It can be cheerful or tense, funny or serious, or maybe some of each, but there needs to be an emotional element that is obvious enough that the reader can recognize it and connect it to their own daily thoughts and lives.
- **Have a defined focus or "angle."** The word "angle" is a journalism term that is synonymous with theme. It is the approach and the direction of the story. This means that the story needs to have an organized thought process that the reader can follow. There should be an emphasis on some aspect of the story that runs throughout the story. Having a well-defined angle will often make it relatively easy to create the story's mood.
  - Example: I was asked recently to write a feature story on a highly successful high school football coach who was retiring at the end of the season. After doing my initial research, which included talking to two of his former players who were now college coaches and also the reporter who regularly covered the coach's team, I realized that most of all this coach was a family man. When I was interviewing the coach and asking routine questions about his family, I discovered that he and his wife had three daughters but no sons. It became apparent that the coach's players were, in effect, the sons he never had. That became the angle of the story: *The coach is not just retiring, he's saying so long to his football "sons."* Because of this choice of an angle, I knew the mood of the story would be a little bittersweet, which was appropriate because as much as the coach was looking forward to spending more time traveling with his wife, he knew he would deeply miss being a coach and he, as well as others interviewed for the story, said they were unsure what would be able to replace football in his daily life.

Together, the **mood** and the **angle** combine to create a story's **central theme.** It has been suggested by more than one literary type that there are only a few central themes in all of literature and that they are just replayed over and over. In a general sense, I would agree wholeheartedly. Some of these basic themes are: Good vs. Evil, Love for thy Mother (or father, or brother or sister), and Triumphing over Adversity. Steve Rushin once noted in a biting "Air and Space" column in *Sports Illustrated* that all sports stories are about either Redemption or Revenge. The point is, make it clear to the reader what your theme is. The best way to emphasize your theme and to make it seem more than a cliché is to . . .

- **Provide deeper insight.** The feature story should tell more about the surroundings, situations and motivational influences behind the story than was previously known.
  - Example: In the story about the retiring high school football coach, I described his cramped basement office and how books of poetry shared shelf space alongside volumes on coaching football. I felt this demonstrated that he wasn't concerned with personal status (the tiny basement office) and that he wasn't all football, all the time (poetry books). When the coach made several clear references to his overall uneasiness with having a story written about him because he was afraid it would detract from the achievements of the players, I made sure to include his apprehensive attitude. I felt it illustrated his deep attachment to his football-playing "sons" and his belief that the team always mattered more than any one individual, even the coach.

This type of detail and personal insight is gained primarily in the interview process. The sportswriter must be aware of more than just the spoken word. Look at the surroundings. What do they say about the interview subject? Watch the person to see how they respond non-verbally to a question or a situation. Do they laugh? Do they grimace? Are they comfortable or uncomfortable with the whole process?

Good, thorough reporting techniques generate the details and impressions that are needed to create a good feature story. Good reporting will also occasionally uncover rare gems of information the sportswriter was unaware of which can totally change the thrust of a story. These gems will not always be pretty. They can, in fact, be quite ugly. An example of this was when *Sports Illustrated* decided to do a feature story on young, exuberant Atlanta Braves relief pitcher John Rocker following the 1999 baseball season. What the *Sports Illustrated* reporter uncovered was that Rocker was quite willing to express racist and hateful opinions about both teammates and people in general. All of us have bits of the good, the bad and the ugly in our personalities. When the overwhelming trait of a profile subject's personality is ugly—and it is verified by the subject's own words and actions and the words of others, as was the case with the Rocker story—then that is what should be written.

Recognizing the rare gems

Fortunately, not all of the gems of information discovered by sportswriters are cast with a negative light. Most, in fact, will provide an effective sparkle to your stories. A gem is finding out something specific about the feature person or team that makes it unique or interesting. The trick is being able to recognize the gem when it comes up during the course of reporting the story and then to mine the gem for all it's worth. It might be some type of statistical trend that has previously been overlooked but is extremely good at explaining why a person or team is successful or not. More often, though, it will be a piece of information that is discovered during an interview.

Here's an example of how a gem of information can be the key to unlocking a great story. Every year in New Hampshire, 33 high school seniors are chosen to represent their state in the Shrine All-Star football game against Vermont. Because the game has been played for nearly 50 years, is for a good cause (Shriners' children's hospitals), and is quite an honor for the players, newspapers across both states routinely do several stories about the players chosen for the game. There were times, however, when we knew relatively little about the players, particularly if they were linemen. That was the case one year when I went to a pre-game dinner/reception held to honor the team. My intent was to interview the New Hampshire coach and the players from our local area to get quotes for a straightforward preview. Right at the end of a conversation with one player, a lineman from a successful, smaller school team who had been overshadowed by his own teammates, he mentioned his only regret was that his dad had died during his sophomore year and would not be able to see him play in the Shrine Game. Here was the gem. It may seem mean-spirited to view a family's misfortune as a reporter's treasure but in writing tragedy is a powerful tool. With a few more follow-up questions, I found out the player and his dad had always used football as their special child-parent bond and together they had dreamed about the son playing in the Shrine Game. Now I had a central theme, with emotional power, that even a non-sports fan could relate to. Here was a son honoring the memory of his father and fulfilling a life-long goal. To add depth to the son's story I made sure to call his mother who supplied needed information about the father and gave another perspective on what the Shrine Game meant to her son. I also went back to the coach and asked some more questions about the player. I had to work a little harder but it was worth it. Instead of a rather bland story full of quotes about how "We really want to beat Vermont" and "We've really been working hard in practice," I had a story that could make readers interested in the event because of the empathy they would feel for the young man.

Feature Story Construction

While a game story will often follow the old inverted pyramid approach of cramming as much information into the opening paragraphs as possible, a good feature story will often take a more deliberate approach. This can be compared to a diamond, instead of a flipped over pyramid **(Figure 15)**. Another way of thinking about it is this: Start with one detail that sets the tone, then build gradually to the core of the story. This will be the majority of the story—the fattest part of a diamond—and will include most of the quotes from the people you have interviewed, along with detailed descriptions of what the sportswriter has witnessed. The quotes and descriptions should reinforce the central theme but also will be used to ex-

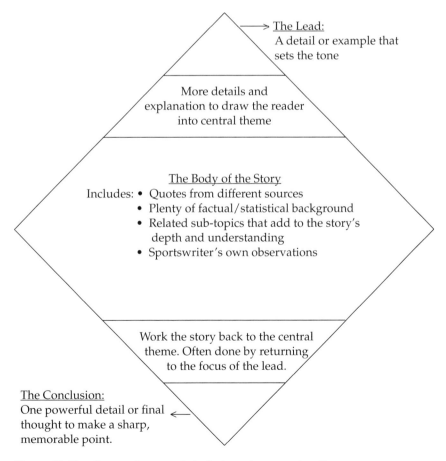

Figure 15: The diamond approach to feature story construction

plain any other topics or issues that are important. This is also where the background behind the story is explained and any supporting facts and figures are generally placed. Then work your way back into an emphasis on the central theme of your story before finishing the story with one particularly telling detail or a final thought, often in the form of a single sentence. Like the story's beginning, the conclusion in a diamond format should form a sharp, distinctive point that has a real impact.

Time is also a key component of a feature story. By this I mean that the descriptions and details that make up a feature story will usually span an extended period of time (an athlete's entire life, the last 20 years of professional baseball, the past two seasons for a successful team). In a game story, almost everything the sportswriter is discussing took place the previous day (or at least in the very recent past). One reason feature stories are such good reads is that this historical information and background make the story more understandable and, ideally, more interesting to the reader.

Examples of the extended time span in feature stories:

- A feature on one athlete should explain where the athlete grew up, how they came to their certain sport, who helped the athlete to achieve, and how they have done in past seasons or events.
- A feature on a team or a group needs to explain how the team/group came together and how their current efforts set them apart from their past as well as other teams.
- Enterprise stories on trends and innovations will almost always begin with a description that characterizes the trend Then the story will take a historical look to explain what the sport used to be like and how it has changed or evolved. Then the story will return to the current trend and make conclusions on the trend's impact.
- Features that intend to preview an event must deal with three distinct time ranges: the past (how the person/team has done), the present (how the person/team is feeling right now), and the future (a prediction of how the person/team will do in the upcoming event).

The notion of a diamond format of story structure is very helpful when dealing with the extended time element of a story. A good general rule is to start with the present when making the sharp point of the lead, get to the historical past in the larger middle of the story to provide the

UNH Women's Dream Team—15 Years Later
Every day,
Karen Geromini
looks at the clock by her door
and remembers the time of her life,
a time her old teammate Barb Marois finds hard to believe.

For Sandy Bridgeman, the memories brought her back to Durham with hopes that a minor women's sport can once again bring UNH a special kind of national prestige, the type it earned 15 years ago for the first time and hasn't received since.

In 1985 those three women were on a lacrosse team that won the university's only NCAA championship. The women's ice hockey team won its sport's first national tournament in 1998 but women's ice hockey is not under NCAA auspices. The men's hockey team came close in 1999, losing in overtime in the final to bitter rival Maine. Several other UNH programs have competed in NCAA tournaments—field hockey, football, gymnastics, volleyball—but only one group of women can truly claim they were number one.

"Everything just came together for us in that one season and that's the sense we had in that season," says Marois.

"And we weren't afraid," Geromini adds.

The team consisted of women from two very distinct athletic backgrounds. First were the lacrosse players, most of whom had learned the game at tony New England prep schools. Then came the field hockey players.

"There were probably eight of us who had never played lacrosse before," Marois says. "We were just recruited into playing."

Forging the two groups together, through intense practices and almost manic conditioning was Marisa Didio, a young, iron-willed coach.

It's now apparent that Didio had plenty of raw material with which to create a high-speed team of diamonds in the rough that put the traditional powers on their ear. It was the greatest collection of women's athletic talent UNH has ever seen.

Marois would go on to be a 10-year member of the U.S. field hockey team, playing in the 1988 and 1996 Olympics, serving as captain for "six or seven of those years," she recalls.

Bridgeman, whose maiden name is Vander-Heyden, was also on the 1988 Olympic field hockey team, her third year on the national team. Geromini and Mary Rogers were members of the national lacrosse team. Goalie Robin Balducci is now the head coach of the women's field hockey team.

"The 1985 team was a group of super athletes," Bridgeman says. "Although a number of us were not great in terms of lacrosse experience, there were a large number that were great team athletes. Great team players. It was a very unselfish team and we just wanted to win."

Their playing style emphasized power, speed and aggressiveness. Despite an appearance in the NCAA tournament the year before, when it was a 12-team tournament, the Wildcats were seen as outsiders when they received the final spot in 1985 after beating Massachusetts to win the ECAC tournament.

In '85 the NCAA lacrosse tournament was pared down to just four teams, with top-rated Temple seen as the favorite. After all, Temple would host UNH,

Figure 16: An example of a story that uses the diamond format to address an extended time period.

then get to play the final in its hometown at Philadelphia's venerable Franklin Field.

Temple had won 29 straight games. When the game ended, a traveling UNH fan unfurled a banner that read "29-1," Bridgeman recalls. The Wildcats had pulled their first upset.

But the Wildcats were still treated with a lack of respect, or at least that's how Marois and Geromini remember it. Both women relate a story that they admit might have been nothing more than a rumor—that UNH had been left out of the final program. Or at the least the program had to be redone because it had been assumed Temple would advance.

Whether the story was true or not, it served a purpose. "It fueled the fire for a lot of us," Marois says.

Maryland was the final opponent and UNH pulled out a 6-5 win. Angie Sherer, who started at UNH as a tennis player, scored the winning goal in the final minutes. The game ended with the ball in Balducci's possession after one last save.

Fifteen years later, the memories of success are still strong, still motivating.

Geromini is now the athletic director and field hockey coach at Thayer Academy in Braintree, MA. When the team was inducted into UNH's Hall of Honor a few years ago, each player was given a clock commemorating the national championship. Geromini says it's the only memento from her two-sport athletic career on display in her home. "That's something I'm very, very proud of," she says.

Marois literally traveled the world via her athletic talent. But what she and her college teammates accomplished still resonates. "It seems even more amazing now. Fifteen years later and it's still the only one and we were lucky enough to say we were there."

Didio resigned to concentrate on field hockey after the '85 season. Marge Anderson took over as head coach and the program remained competitive for a few years—including a Final Four appearance in 1986.

Like many other programs at UNH, the practice of getting by on the minimum—something the 1985 team did splendidly—caught up to the Wildcats. With no scholarships and increasingly fewer scholarship athletes crossing over to play lacrosse, power was replaced by mediocrity. Then came a part-time coach right out of college making chump change. The team was in disarray when Bridgeman took over.

"Memories of that year, winning the championship, played a great part in the feeling of this is where I want to be," Bridgeman says.

In her first year as coach, UNH went 4-10. The past two seasons have seen 7-8 and 8-8 records with losses in the America East conference semifinals both years. But the team is now allotted six scholarships, half the NCAA maximum.

In 2001 the America East tournament champion will receive an automatic bid to the NCAA tournament. UNH is still an underdog but now they are beginning to be an underdog with some bite.

Just like they were

15 years ago.

(Written by Steve Craig. Reprinted with permission from New Hampshire Magazine, June 2000)

Figure 16: Continued

needed background and depth, and then return to the present (or make a future prediction) in the sharp, final point of the conclusion. **(Figure 16 is an example of a present-past-present story.)**

Another approach to story structure, which is similar to the diamond format, can be summed up by the phrase "Small Picture-Big Picture-Small Picture." While it can be applied to many types of feature stories, this is an especially useful method when it comes to enterprise stories, where the objective of the story is to explain a widespread situation, problem, or trend.

"Small Picture" means a single case or person that is being affected or impacted by the "Big Picture," with the Big Picture being the farther-reaching situation, trend or innovation that the story is about. Starting with a Small Picture accomplishes two things: 1. it helps to explain the effect or impact of the Big Picture and 2. it personalizes the Big Picture, by giving it an immediate human face and reference.

After the reader sees a Small Picture of the problem then it will be easier to discuss the many variables and details that have caused the Big Picture situation to develop. After that description is completed the sportswriter returns the reader to the Small Picture, often by means of the original group or person, to give the conclusion a personalized feel.

Summary on Feature Stories

Continually ask yourself three key questions while writing a feature story, regardless of its style or purpose.

1. Am I connecting the story to a central theme that the reader can understand?
2. Am I using enough details and descriptions to support my central theme and to add to the reader's understanding and enjoyment of the article?
3. Have I talked to every possible person (in the time I have left before deadline) who can add a different or more insightful perspective to this story? This is a question you should ask with any story you are writing.

Chances are you will often answer "No" to these questions. When you do, try to improve on what you're writing, or make another phone call. You may not ever quite get to perfection (I haven't yet) but each time you address a need in the story, you will be making it stronger.

CHAPTER 8

What is a Sidebar Story?

The word "sidebar" is a journalistic term for a story that accompanies a major news story. As it applies to sports writing it is often used as a catchall phrase to describe, in part, how an event is going to be covered.

If a newspaper is going to cover a major sporting event, be it the Super Bowl or a state high school championship game, it is going to produce more than one story. The sports editor will decide beforehand how much space will be devoted to the overall package of stories and then will give the assembled staff a general direction like, "We'll have a game story, a column, and three sidebars, one on the winning team, one on the losing team, and one on the key play or happening of the game." The specifics of the sidebar stories, however, are usually decided during or immediately after the game. The action of the game determines what will be the central themes of the sidebars.

In a perfect sports world, that means there will be at least three sportswriters assigned to the event: One will write the game story, one will be the assigned column writer, and the other will be the lead sidebar writer.

The purpose of sidebars is to detail aspects of the main event that will not be covered extensively in the game story itself. For example, the game story will have some reaction to the outcome from both the winning and losing sides but will primarily describe the action of the game itself. The winning team sidebar will capture the elation of victory and add detail about how and why that team won. The losing team sidebar will explain the pain and suffering of the losing team and why its hopes were dashed. The third sidebar (key play or happening) will require quicker decision-making at the game site and communication between the writers to choose the next-best topic that won't be written about extensively in the game story, column or the other sidebars. The key play is often the winning score, or a particular play that alters the momentum of the game.

The sidebar story takes a small part of the game, event or full-length feature and shapes it into a thorough explanation of why that small part is intregal to the final outcome.

A classic example of the sidebar is using the one key play of the game, interviewing the key parties involved in the play—the coach who called it, the players who executed it or were befuddled by it, maybe a referee or umpire who had to react to it—and then writing a story about how that one key play happened, what its impact was, and how the people involved reacted to it.

Generally, a sidebar story is about 500 words long, which is in the neighborhood of 15 to 18 good-sized paragraphs. (See the "How Long is Long" section in Chapter 5 for a description of story lengths.)

When it comes to the basics of a sidebar, follow these general guidelines:

- Sidebars should be well defined and not try to do too much. If the purpose is to detail the one key play of the game, keep the focus on the play. Do not digress into a multi-paragraph description of one player's family background.
- Often times sidebars can be chosen in general terms before the event (i.e., one on the losing team, one on the winning team) but will need to be refined with quick decision-making by the sportswriter as the game is ending.
    - Example: One player on the losing team, a high school senior, plays a truly superior game but comes up short on his final shot to win the game. The sportswriter could go to the losing team and interview several people about a wide array of things that happened in the game and come up with a very general "it feels bad to lose" story. What would be more powerful is to put the emphasis on the one player, detailing both his successes and his unsuccessful final chance, and use him as an example of how a team's valiant effort came up just a little bit short. Chances are his comments will

be the most descriptive as long as he is allowed some private time and the sportswriter is not overly pushy or confrontational.
- If more than one reporter from the same newspaper is covering the game, then sidebars should be discussed by the reporters before they start their post-game interviews to avoid repetition and to use their time as wisely as possible.
  - Example: One person is assigned the game story and the winning team sidebar. The other person is assigned the losing team sidebar. The sportswriter working on the losing team sidebar should ask questions in his interview that will produce responses that can be used for the game story, as well as those that are asked specifically for the losing team sidebar. This can be done much more effectively if the reporter going to the losing team area knows what the game-story writer wants to emphasize.
- Sometimes a sidebar can serve as one person's take on the game, either because they figured prominently in the game or because they are known to be outspoken.
  - Example A: A high school football championship game is won with a last-second field goal and it turns out the field goal kicker is primarily a soccer player who only went out for football in his senior season. While some comment or reaction from the kicker is needed for the game story, the uniqueness of his situation (soccer player turned football player) warrants a separate sidebar on the kicker.
  - Example B: Same game, so what do you write about for the losing team? Especially since the score of the game was 10-7 and no one from the losing team had a superior effort. This is where the sportswriter might seek out a senior who has experience talking to the media, because the sportswriter knows this particular kid can handle being "the voice" in a tough situation.

The manner of writing a sidebar for a game or event is typically a stripped-down version of the feature story but with more emphasis on the post-game reporting than on pre-game research, since the specific angle of the sidebar should be determined by what happens during the game. The purpose is to supplement the coverage of the game by giving the reader additional and differing reactions to the game or event.

Sidebars to Feature Stories

Sometimes sidebars are used to support a major feature, enterprise story, or investigative report. These are designed to highlight a particular person, a key aspect or a specific event that is part of the overall story.

The purpose is much the same as with a game-story sidebar. The sports section is trying to highlight one part of the overall story by displaying it with a separate headline. This is a good way of handling a subtopic to the overall story. The sidebar gives the subtopic its due while at the same time freeing the writer from going into a multi-paragraph explanation that could muddle the flow and clarity of the larger piece. Other times, sidebars are used as a means of giving a personalized example of the overall point of the larger story.

An Example of How Sidebars Can Create a Stronger Overall Presentation

Your sports department has decided to do an in-depth study of how much progress women athletes have made at the local university in the past 10 years. It is a big project and one that would be cumbersome and difficult to grasp for both writer and reader unless it is broken into smaller parts.

Here's an example of how the sports staff might break down the project.

1. An *editorial note.* The purpose of an editorial note is to tell the reader clearly what the newspaper is trying to accomplish. This would probably be at the top of the main story or perhaps be given a separate, easy-to-see space on the page.
2. The main story. This would detail where women athletes were 10 years ago, where they are now, and whether they are being treated fairly and equally compared with the men at the university. The story would be based on statistical comparisons and personal reactions from administrators, coaches and athletes.
3. Sidebar 1. This would give an explanation of Title IX, the law that requires, among other things, that public universities provide fair and equal opportunities for participation in athletics to women. This sidebar would discuss what the law does require and also common misconceptions about what it states.
4. Sidebar 2. It is important to personalize issue-oriented report-

ing. Write a human interest story that details how one athlete or coach has benefited from advancements at the university.
5. Sidebar 3. Chances are that other women do not feel they have benefited from the changes, so write a human interest story that details how one athlete feels she has been mistreated or not given equal benefit because she is a woman.
6. A statistical graphic. This would be used to compare scholarships, coaches' salaries, number of athletes, number of sports, and facilities used for both men and women.

The main story will certainly have references to Title IX, positive advancements and negative aspects of the overall women's athletic programs. The purposes of sidebars are, respectively, to explain in great detail a complicated law and then to personalize both the university's advancements and its failings. Taken together, the package will give a very complete picture of what it's like to be a woman athlete at the local university, for better or worse.

In the course of reporting the story, other sidebars will probably be added to the list. Perhaps it becomes apparent that one single person was most responsible for changing the way the university approached and supported women's athletics. If so, that person could merit a separate story, detailing his or her achievements. Or it becomes clear that the university chose to eliminate one or more men's sports in order to balance its overall athletic budget and participation numbers between women's and men's athletics. If so, a sidebar on the male athletes' reaction to losing their sports would be in order.

CHAPTER 9

The Beat Writer's Notebook

There is one aspect of sports writing that I have not discussed in much detail. **Sports writing is entertaining and fun**—for the sportswriter and especially for the readers.

It's my opinion that there is nothing wrong with recognizing that sports are a great form of entertainment and sports writing should therefore be entertaining. One of the best stylistic methods for both entertaining and informing the sports fan is through the type of story called "the notebook".

Before discussing the key aspects of writing a notebook-style story, three definitions are needed.

A *beat* is a specific area of coverage assigned to one reporter. There are many different types of beats. Sports sections, depending on their size, will have separate beats for professional sports teams, major college teams, high school sports, and specific sports.

A *beat writer* is the reporter assigned to cover a beat, which in sports writing is usually a specific team, event or sport.

A *beat writer's notebook* is several different pieces of information put together in a package presented as one story. The information will deal with several different topics or themes, usually separated by small, bold headlines referred to as subheads. While a notebook routinely deals with at least three different topics (sometimes a dozen or more), all will have a connection to a specific team, event, or sport. Most often, notebooks are written by a beat writer.

The best-known examples of beat writers are found at big-city newspapers that extensively cover professional sports teams. Smaller papers also usually have beat writers and they are assigned to areas that are considered to have the greatest local interest.

- Example A: *The Boston Globe* is generally considered to have one of the country's best sports sections, combining first-rate writing with a visually pleasing use of headlines, photographs and graphics to create an excellent presentation. The Boston area is home to professional teams in the four major sports (baseball, football, basketball, hockey) and men's and women's soccer. There are also four well-known universities, numerous smaller colleges, the world's best-known marathon and one of its most famous rowing regattas. All of the beats have year-round responsibilities. The reporters who cover the professional teams write very few stories that are not connected to their team or their team's sport. Other reporters might handle two beats that do not overlap. For many years, the auto racing beat writer has also been the primary reporter covering Boston College. Add in the fact that the *Globe*'s sports section tries to cover sports from a local (Boston and suburbs), regional (New England), national and international perspective, and you can see that there are plenty of different beats that can be created, including:
    - The Boston Red Sox
    - Major League Baseball (separate writer)
    - New England Patriots
    - Boston Celtics
    - Boston Bruins
    - Skiing/Outdoors
    - auto racing
    - New England Revolution soccer
    - Boston College (all sports)
    - college sports (covering most of New England)
    - Olympic sports
    - boxing

- Example B: About an hour's drive to the north of the *Globe* of-

fices is *Foster's Daily Democrat* in Dover, N.H., the daily paper where I worked for over 12 years. Our paper also had beats but they were tailored to the local sports scene. Our greatest emphasis in terms of actual coverage of events was the high school sports scene and the athletic programs at the nearby University of New Hampshire. For many years we had only three beats assigned to our staff writers:
- The University of New Hampshire men's hockey team
- The University of New Hampshire football team
- The University of New Hampshire men's and women's basketball teams (one beat)

Every person on the staff was equally responsible for reporting and covering events at the 20 high schools in our area. We supplemented the sports section by hiring *free-lance writers* to write about special-interest topics of auto racing, hunting and fishing, and outdoor recreation. Free-lance writers are people who are hired by the newspaper for a specific purpose or to provide extra game coverage and are paid on a per-story basis. In the cases of the auto racing and hunting/fishing writers, they were individuals who had significant expertise and experience in the fields they were writing about. When a super speedway was built in New Hampshire in the early 1990s, the free-lance auto racing writer was replaced by a full-time staff writer whose major responsibility from April until October was to cover auto racing.

Becoming a beat writer is a privilege and a sign of respect. It is also a significant responsibility. The beat writer becomes the paper's expert on a certain team or sport and both editors and readers expect the beat writer to be better informed than the most avid fan.

In major newspaper markets this is an extremely grueling and competitive position. There is often more than one major daily newspaper in the same city with at least some medium-sized dailies from the suburbs also in competition. Each paper has its own beat writers, each writer is after the same stories, and all are trying to get the story first.

The beat writer's primary responsibility is to cover the team and its games. That means the beat writer is responsible for writing the game stories and reporting on the important news surrounding a team or a sport (trades, hirings/firings, injuries). In the process of doing these things, the beat writer routinely comes up with information that is not directly related to last night's game, or is not important enough to warrant its own separate story, or that needs a little more explanation. Still, these bits of information are interesting and should be presented to the reader. They are placed together in a catchall story called the notebook.

Therefore, the notebook contains facts and tidbits of information that an expert (the beat writer) considers to be important, interesting, and entertaining. These should be the juicy updates that a fan can't wait to devour. Common notebook items are:

- Who's hot?
- Which players are in a slump?
- Which players are injured and won't play?
- Which players are injured but will play anyway?
- Are any players complaining about a lack of playing time?
- Who's likely to be traded or demoted?
- How is the No. 1 draft pick doing in the minors?
- What does an opposing coach, player or scout have to say about the team?
- What funny thing did the team comedian say about last night's game?

Taken individually, the tidbits have only limited usefulness and probably would not warrant the space they would take on a sports page if each had to have its own separate headline. Packaged together, they make for informative and entertaining reading.

Think of it this way: Imagine the information as toys, the notebook story is a box, and the reader is a curious child. If the toys are just scattered all over the floor, all you have is a big mess and the child will probably pick up one toy and ignore the rest. But if you put all the toys in one attractive toy box, the child will be drawn to the box like a magnet to metal and will instinctively sort through the entire box to discover all of its hidden treasures.

Readers of the sports section learn that the notebook story is like a wonderful toy box. It is worth their time to discover the treasures of information it holds.

How a Beat Writer Gets Great Notebook Information

Reporting.

In a word, reporting is how a good notebook story is created. Beat writers spend most of their working time talking to people connected to the team or sport they have been assigned to. It's called **establishing and maintaining contacts.** The word *contacts* is often used synonymously for the word *sources*. The only difference really is that the word "contacts," as it is used in journalism, refers only to people. The term "sources" in journalism usually means people but also includes research material like newspaper and magazine articles, Web sites, court records, and reference books.

Establishing contacts means getting to know the people who make a difference on a team or in a sport as well as getting to know the people who can help you to understand what the differences really mean. When a person is a contact, that means the sportswriter can talk to that person and expect to get valuable information for a story. Since no contact is qualified or willing to be a source of information for every story, the sportswriter needs to develop a wide range of contacts among the athletes, coaches, team owners and administrators as well as from the groups of people who work behind the scenes—people like the guy who passes out equipment, the athletic trainers, scouts, player agents, well-connected alumni, and influential business people. Parents can become invaluable contacts. Even fans can sometimes be useful contacts if they have a personal relationship with someone connected to the team.

Having contacts is one thing. Using them is the key. For the beat writer that usually takes the shape of a standard routine. The sportswriter makes sure that certain people are contacted on a regular basis, through planned meetings and expected phone calls. If it's been awhile since you've seen or talked with a good contact, then give them a call just to say hello. It's polite, it makes the contact feel liked, it's professional on the part of the reporter and more times than not it will generate something useful and probably unexpected.

When I was the beat writer for the University of New Hampshire football team I definitely had a routine, or what could be called a schedule. Below is an example of what could be considered just a typical afternoon of work, where I interact with six distinct contacts. Notice how tidbits of information accumulate and how they will be used in a notebook story.

1. Regular weekly meeting with the coach. The primary purpose of the meeting is to interview the coach for two preview stories, one emphasizing how UNH matched up with that Saturday's opponent, the other featuring a specific UNH player. During the interview it becomes apparent the coach is still upset with what he views as poor officiating in the previous game. "There were two holding calls against us that on the film were absolutely not holding," the coach says. There's **Notebook Item**

No. 1: *Coach upset with officials.* I'll supplement his comment by explaining which specific calls he's referring to and what impact the calls had on last week's game. Injuries are a big part of football. Every week I would get an update on the injury status of key players. Most of this information would go in the overall game preview. On this occasion, the coach also informs me that a player who was a projected starter in preseason but has already missed the first seven weeks of the season is now beginning to do some light exercising. Since the player won't be back for this week, or probably the season, that information is not for the game preview. Still, news of his progress is important enough for **Notebook Item No. 2.**

The coach is in his 24th season at the school, so when he says that "Jim Concannon's hit on their big tight end last week was about as fierce as any hit I've seen on this field," it's a comment that's worth printing. There's **Notebook Item No. 3.**

It's a good idea to try to plan the top or lead item in your notebook stories just as you would any other story. As an experienced reporter, I've noticed a trend. Most of the teams in the league now have pass-oriented offenses, where just a few years ago almost every team relied on the running game. Ideally, I've identified this trend and decided I would use it as a Notebook lead *before* I meet with the head coach. It's possible I might come across something better to use as the lead item but by identifying my priority item beforehand, I'm prepared to ask some questions about why the league has become pass-happy. Since the coach is one of my most knowledgeable sources when it comes to the actual strategies and details of football, I ask him his opinion. He says, "I really think it runs in cycles. A few years ago, everybody wanted to run the ball, so teams went out and recruited big, strong defensive linemen and linebackers who could stuff the run. Now teams can't run the ball, so they have to come up with something different. Now it's up to the defenses to react." That confirms what I felt was the case and that's **Notebook Item No. 4.** I'll expand on this with other sources.

2. Head coach's secretary. A wonderful person, she is adept at warning me if the coach is in a foul mood. She also is a good source for phone numbers of the players and information about former players. This week she lets me know that a former UNH star now playing in the NFL has called ahead for tickets and plans to attend Saturday's game. This could be a notebook item but I store this one away, not wanting to alert other writers to a possible story. I will try to interview the player sometime before or after Saturday's game. The conversation doesn't generate a notebook item but it does produce useful information and another possible story.

3. **Assistant coaches.** I made specific appointments with assistant coaches when I knew I needed to talk to them for several minutes. More frequently, I would just make it a point to engage them in conversation whenever possible. They often would give me a better read on who was playing well and who was not, since the head coach would only criticize players' performances publicly if he thought it would motivate them to play better. In talking to the defensive backs coach I discover that one of the cornerbacks has been playing on a bad ankle all season that is only now starting to feel better. Because the player has not missed any games, the injury hasn't been reported previously. "He's moving better than he has since the first week of preseason," the assistant coach says. **Notebook Item No. 5** is quickly jotted down. I then ask the defensive backs coach for his take on how to slow down the pass-happy offenses around the league, to expand **Notebook Item No. 4.**

Talking with the offensive line coach we begin to discuss a sophomore who has recently cracked the lineup. "You wouldn't believe how strong this kid is. And it's all natural. He grew up on a dairy farm in upstate New York. The kid had never been in a weight room before he came here and he's already bench-pressing 400 pounds." This folksy comment about UNH's own farm boy becomes **Notebook Item No. 6.**

4. **The trainer's room.** Coaches can tell you who is hurt but chances are they don't know the exact nature of an injury. That's why I always tried to seek out the team's athletic trainer to get the particulars. The athletic trainer is the person in charge of day-to-day health concerns of the team, helping to heal bumps and bruises as well as overseeing recovery from more serious injuries. I was careful to quote him only on injury-related topics. I did not want to ruin my relationship with him and, very importantly, I wanted to maintain free access to the trainer's room. It was a convenient spot to talk with players in a relatively relaxed atmosphere. (It's hard for them to get away while they're in the middle of having an ankle taped). On this day, two key players are receiving some extra treatment: the star running back who sprained his knee a few weeks ago and a linebacker who had been named the league's defensive player of the week. Comments from the players on their injury and award, respectively, give me **Notebook items No. 7 and 8.** I also spend some time talking to the linebacker about the increased amount of passing offense in the league and how it affects the way he has to play his position. "You can't be as reckless, that's for sure. It was a whole lot easier—and a lot more fun— when I knew that eight out of 10 plays I was going to be trying to knock down a running back. You have to think more, and that takes away some of your aggressiveness." That's a great comment for **Notebook item No.**

4, because it shows the effect pass-oriented offenses can have on a defensive player's approach to the game.

     5. Attending practices. This is the beat writer's opportunity to use his or her own eyes to check things out. Let's say UNH has been having some trouble moving the ball on offense. On this day I notice the backup quarterback is working with the first team. Is there a quarterback switch in store? This is not a notebook item, at least not yet. This requires another question to the head coach who failed to mention anything about a QB switch in our interview three hours earlier. If the team really is starting a different quarterback on Saturday then it should be its own story. Instead, the coach claims the second-string QB is just getting a "little extra work" with the first team but will not start. If I feel the coach is being straightforward, then it probably is not worth a separate story but should be reported. I choose to believe the coach, especially when the regular starter returns to the first unit for the final half of the practice. This is **Notebook Item No. 9.**

     6. Media Relations staff. Except for coaches and sportswriters, few people know this group of people even exist but they are extremely helpful. This is where I get the updated statistics for UNH and hopefully the statistics for this week's opponent and the rest of the teams in the league. There are always a couple of statistics worth using. I take a look at the stats package and notice that through seven games the star running back has 920 yards rushing, meaning he could go over 1,000 yards (an accepted milestone) this Saturday with just an ordinary game. There's **Notebook item No. 10.** I would always take the time to talk to the Media Relations staff. Members of this profession will usually know quite a bit about the inner workings of a team or athletic department. Of course, they are also employed by the team or organization, so the information they are willing to release may be limited to the basics.

     You can see that the notebook items can quickly pile up. This is just one afternoon of work and I haven't even interviewed the player I'm going to do the feature preview on yet, or included any notes gained from a discussion earlier in the week with the opposing team's head coach.

Putting the Notebook Together

Once a sportswriter has a bundle of information for a notebook, it's time to organize the information. As a general rule, you start with the most newsworthy item and work down to the least important, perhaps mixing in a funny or humorous story along the way.

After reviewing my notes, I'm going to stick with my original, planned thought to have a mini-analysis of the league's increased fondness for the pass offense as the top item in the notebook. This was **Notebook Item No. 4** as I acquired them during reporting. The comments from the assistant coach and linebacker are added to the head coach's comment. I back up my assertion that teams are passing the ball more and forcing defenses to change the way they play with league-wide statistics comparing the past three seasons (available in media guides I have at the office).

Since I'm talking about pass offenses and pass defense, I'll follow this with a sub-head titled **"DBs fight back,"** and use **Items No. 3** and **5,** in that order. Here I'll say that the best way to slow down any offense is to smack them around a bit, as Jim Concannon did last week, and then use the quote from the head coach. Then I would comment that the cornerback with the bad ankle is apt to play better and use the quote from the defensive backs coach. In this case, I've gone against my "most newsworthy" rule because **Notebook Items No. 3** and **5** are connected to my lead discussion.

For my third section, now I'll be sure to choose the most newsworthy item, which is the hint of a quarterback switch **(Item No. 9)** under a sub-head that might read **"Who's passing whom?"** Here I would describe how much the second-team QB worked out with the first team, why a switch might be in order (the regular starter's stats and the team's performance with him in control) and then use the coach's comment denying that there will be a switch this week.

My fourth section starts with the sub-head **"The 1,000-yard march."** Here I'll state the obvious, that the star running back needs 80 yards to reach the 1,000-yard rushing mark, which was **Item No. 10.** I'll add the quote about how he's adapting to playing with an injury **(Item No. 7).** Then I'll analyze what he's done in the past two games while playing hurt. Come to find out, he averaged an excellent 149 yards per game in the first five games but a much more ordinary 87.5 yards since being hurt. This way, the reader knows about both the milestone and the running back's relative drop-off in production.

The sixth section is entitled **"Life on the Farm"** and is the relatively good-natured anecdote about the big, strong offensive lineman **(Item No. 6).**

I still have three distinct items left: the coach complaining about the officials, the injured update on the player who has missed the whole season, and the linebacker commenting on his award. None is particularly strong, so I might just group them under a general subhead that readers would recognize as the end segment of my notebook. Since the University of New Hampshire's nickname is the Wildcats, I could use something cute like **'Cat tracks:** or something simple like the word **Notes:**

All told, the reader has been given a good story. There's an analysis of a league-wide trend, the whiff of a quarterback controversy, a quick take on the star running back's recent efforts, along with two or three interesting quotes.

When is a Notebook Item Not a Notebook Item?

A sportswriter may be looking for just a little tidbit when a real story shows up. In the above example there were a couple of cases where if the information I received had been even slightly different, I would have had to treat a notebook item as its own separate story.

The obvious one was the quarterback controversy. I chose to put my faith in the coach's word, especially when the regular starter returned to the first unit later in the practice. What would have happened if the regular starter had spent the whole day with the second team? Then, regardless of what the coach says, it's a bigger story. I would have needed to interview the two quarterbacks along with other players—a captain, an experienced offensive lineman, the team's top receiver—to get their reactions to the starter spending a day demoted to the second team. **The reason newspapers have beat writers is that they can get timely news stories.** It's the beat writer's job to understand when he or she sees or hears something that is so newsworthy that it demands its own story and the headline that goes with it.

There were several other instances where I had to make a judgment as to how newsworthy a particular piece of information was. Remember the coach complaining about the officiating? I ended up using it at the tail end of the notebook, not granting it much importance at all. What if he had followed up his one comment by saying, "That was the worst officiated game I've ever seen and I've made a formal complaint to the league office"? Then it becomes a legitimate story. In fact, the UNH coach did say something to that effect once, and I spent most of the rest of the day finding out how the league would respond to the head coach's complaints and if he could be fined or sanctioned for his comments. I also learned (and then explained) how officials are assigned to games, who assigns them, and how they are graded or judged.

You might remember that I learned that an NFL player and former UNH star would be on campus Saturday but decided to hold that news so I could interview him, hopefully undistracted by other media. By making that decision, I've given myself an extra assignment on the day of the game. Now it's my responsibility to alert my editor of my intentions (so they can plan a spot for the story) and to make sure I actually get the interview and then create a story.

What if the star running back says he doesn't think he can play this Saturday and that he shouldn't have been playing the week before? Then it's a major controversy, since the player is implying that the school's medical staff is not acting in his best interests, and the sportswriter's work really begins.

You are never 'on' the team

One of the more difficult aspects of being a beat writer is making sure that you stay objective in your reporting. Being objective means that a reporter needs to report both sides of a single story and both sides of the ongoing story. As a beat writer, that means there will be times you will have to write a story that you know will be upsetting to the team you are covering. The best thing to remember in that situation is that **a sportswriter's loyalties should be with their own team—the newspaper or magazine they work for.** *A sportswriter is not "on" a sports team. You may be on the road with the Boston Red Sox from mid-February until early-October. You may talk with Pedro Martinez more than you do your best friend but you are still not "part" of the Red Sox organization.*

Usually when it comes to the really big issues, the sportswriter will not hesitate to write what is needed. What does happen, based on my observations and personal experience, is that beat writers tend to pick out certain favorites within a team. They do it almost subconsciously. Their favorites tend to be the players and coaches who are open with them and have been "good quotes." (A "good quote" is a person who can be counted on to be available before or after a game and has the ability to sum up a situation in lively, descriptive language.) When that player makes a bad play, there is a tendency to let it slide and not mention it in the story. That's a mistake of omission, meaning the sportswriter left out an important detail. Or, a sportswriter might always make sure to get their favorite's side of a controversy but are not as diligent when it comes to one of the players they dislike, have had disagreements with, or perhaps have never bothered to speak to in the past.

When it comes to your writing and reporting, keep yourself in check by continually asking, "Am I doing this because it's the right thing for a sportswriter to do or because it's what the members of the team I'm covering would want me to do?"

One other thing. **There is no cheering in the press box.** *Inwardly, you may be rooting for your local team to win the big game. It's only natural. After all, you have gotten to know the players and coaches. Just keep your mouth shut when you're in the press box. That is a place for objective reporters, possibly from all over the country. Start cheering for a certain team or player and you will immediately label yourself as a complete amateur.*

Here are Five Good Rules to Follow When Compiling a Notebook:

1. Start with the most important news.
2. As you are writing the notebook, continually ask yourself if a particular topic needs to be addressed in greater detail. If it does, chances are it does not belong in a notebook format but as a separate story.
3. Indicate a new topic by using subheads.
4. Keep each topic or item relatively short. It helps maintain a fast-paced, information-first format. If a particular topic is going on for more than six or seven paragraphs, then that's another indicator that you have a legitimate stand-alone story.
5. Notebooks should be informative *and* entertaining.

Sports sections have for years been referred to as the toy shop or the candy store inside a newspaper. These are meant as unflattering slams, with the strong implication that being a sportswriter or sports editor is easy and does not require any amount of expertise. There is a bit of truth in the otherwise flawed characterization, especially if you look at the sports section from the reader's point of view. Sports are organized forms of play. Even the most highly paid athletes are usually happiest when they are playing their sport. Sports are supposed to be fun and they still are for a great many people.

Beat writer's notebook stories are a great way to add to the entertainment value of a sports section because they offer a nice mix of news, quotes, and expert opinion from the reporter who is an expert observer.

CHAPTER 10

The Column

In some ways, not much has changed in more than 2,000 years. Where sports are played, there are quite often sportswriters watching the action and offering a whole lot of opinions. They talk about what went right or wrong, who is good or bad, who they like, who they don't.

I believe all sportswriters think that way. We're constantly evaluating players and performers on the basis of accepted standards of performance (points, goals, batting average, shooting percentage, etc.). We're also constantly making personal judgments about a player or coach. Everything from the way they wear their uniform ("Those knee-high socks have gotta go.") to their post-game attitude ("He/she was a good/boring/jerk interview.") is evaluated.

Many of us talk that way, making our opinions known during a game, either to friends, fans or fellow sportswriters.

Only a few sportswriters, however, get to write their stories that way.

These sportswriters are called **Sports Columnists**, usually the best-paid writers on the staff. They are paid well because their opinions and judgments presumably create greater interest in the sports pages.

When a sportswriter's opinions go from their head to the computer and ultimately on to the printed page it's called a sports column. It should probably be referred to as The Column, with an upper case T and

C because these are the best-read, most talked about stories in almost any sports section.

By definition, a ***sports column*** is a story based upon the writer's opinion. In that way it is distinctly different from any other type of story. In fact, good columns need to choose a side: For or Against; Good or Bad; Right or Wrong; Strong or Weak.

It is the oldest style of sports writing. In the age of the ancient Olympics (roughly 776 B.C.–AD 396), Greek scholars, poets and musicians all took turns playing sportswriter, voicing their opinions of both the athletes and the overall level of competition. At times they were highly critical in their opinions. Others tried to glorify an athlete's accomplishment, comparing it to some grander endeavor or the acts of the gods themselves.

It's the same thing today. Sports columnists essentially fall into three basic groups when it comes to their styles, or approaches, to column writing: the cheerleader, the critic, and the teacher.

The cheerleader is also sometimes called a "homer," as in a writer who always thinks the home or local team is the best. They overlook flaws or mistakes in an effort, make excuses (usually provided by the coach) for losses, and over-glorify relatively small victories. Very few columnists would ever willingly admit to being a cheerleader. Still, almost all columnists have written columns that essentially shout the praises for a particular individual or team. The difference is that a good columnist makes sure there is a good reason to salute someone or some team. For the most part, the cheerleader columnist is found at small newspapers, usually writing about high school sports.

The critic's primary purpose is to judge an event, player, team or issue. Critics are like movie reviewers; they give thumbs-up or thumbs-down opinions on current events or issues in the sports world. Quite often the critic sports columnist will be adept at using humor. This can take the form of sarcasm (a harsher, biting form of language that is usually used to make fun of someone or something) or light-hearted, gentle wit. The critic often targets athletes, coaches, owners, or aspects of the sports world he or she sees as unjust. Professional athletes and coaches are increasingly easy targets for the critic, in part because almost any newspaper reader carries a bit of jealousy toward someone making millions of dollars a year to play a game.

The best sports columnists can float between the two extremes of critic and cheerleader. These are the teachers. They use a wide array of language tools, ranging from the harshest sarcasm to the sweetest praise, as a means of teaching a lesson through their interpretations of the sporting events they witness. The teaching columnist's objective is to make a point and to show readers why the columnist's opinions about the meaning of an event are justified.

Columns can be written on almost any topic. Since they are usually accompanied by the column writer's picture, they are also easy to spot on a page. Columns can be combined with the coverage of a game or news event or can be a completely separate topic.

Whether you are a cheerleader, critic or teacher, good column writing requires clear thinking and a commitment to your opinion.

The Eight Commandments of Sports Columns (Figure 17)

1. Always be on the lookout for a juicy topic. By juicy, I don't necessarily mean supermarket tabloid "Grandmother Gives Birth to Alien" juicy. I'm talking about ideas that interest you, as the writer. When you are reporting, talking, writing, showering, whatever, be thinking about your game, feature and preview stories and ask yourself, "How would I write this as a column? Would this make a good column? Do I have a strong opinion about this person/team/issue?" If you come up with a good topic, or even a so-so topic, write it down. Keep a list of topic ideas that you won't lose. It's always good to have extra ideas and to identify the topic ideas that need a little more polishing before they are ready to be turned into a column.

2. Figure out what your point will be. There's nothing harder in sports writing than to try to write a column when you really don't know what it is you're trying to say. A good way to help you figure out the point of a column is to talk about it first. Can you state your point in conversation? Do people understand your point, even if they disagree? If they offer a different opinion, does that change how you feel about an issue?

3. Choose a topic that concerns your readers. Let's say I feel strongly that in professional rodeo, a bull rider should only have to stay on top of the bull for six seconds instead of the eight seconds currently required. I know bulls and bull riders and I'm absolutely sure of what my point is.

Just one very big problem. I happen to be a sportswriter in New Hampshire and there are probably no more than three people in the whole state who care the least bit about rodeos. This column could be the best piece of writing and reporting I've ever done but it would be completely worthless. I totally misjudged what is interesting to the readers.

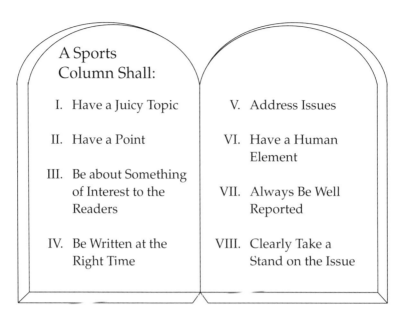

Figure 17: The Eight Commandments of Column Writing

    The surest way to get to know exactly who your readers are is to be out covering events, talking with fans, and living and working in a certain area. That's why top column writing jobs are usually assigned to veteran reporters. They have a trained sense of what is important and what are the hot topics that sports fans want to read about, especially the sports fans in the area where their newspaper is delivered.

    Try to write about things that are routinely the focus of the sports section you are writing for. If you are working for your high school newspaper, then your columns should be about issues that are being talked about in your school and are especially significant to your school: *"School needs better phys. ed. teachers," "Girls deserve as many night games as the boys,"* or *"Add lacrosse as a varsity sport."*

    If you are working for your hometown newspaper which covers Little League to the local college, then those are the places for you to find your column ideas. Some ideas might be similar to what a school newspaper would write but should be broadened, as in *"State needs to increase funding for physical education,"* or *"It's time to let girls shine equally."* Others will be team or sport specific: *"Time to scrap run-and-gun offense for UNH football."*

    The key point is to keep the column topics within the range of what you routinely report on whenever possible. If you're writing a column, you better know what it is you're talking about. It is my opinion that most columns written about professional sports by sportswriters who do not regularly cover the professional sport are uninformed, bland, and have only limited appeal. It is also a sign that the columnist couldn't come up with a good idea that had more local interest (which means they probably need to get out of the office more).

4. Choose the right time. This means to be aware of what is called "timeliness" in the news business. That means certain issues have greater importance during particular seasons of the year and they have the greatest impact when they are connected to a recent or soon-to-happen event. As I said earlier in the chapter, columns are often packaged with other stories, all dealing with the same game or event. In this way, readers get the facts and comments from the game story or the news story and they are offered an opinion in the form of a sports column. So, if the primary news coverage of a sports section is going to be about the opening day of the baseball season, it would be poor timing to write a column about the "out-of-season" local college football team. An exception, however, would be if the local college had just announced that it was going to eliminate its football program. That's a huge news story. In this case a column about the football program (*"Why football should be eliminated/saved"*) is the absolute best choice, whether it's opening day or not.

5. Make your topic issue-oriented. In general, a column will have greater overall impact if its main point is about a certain issue that is important to your readers. The issue can be very broad, as in "T*he importance of choosing right from wrong*," or very specific, as in "T*he local high school needs a new gym*". If you have decided that the point of your story is "T*he senior guard on the local high school basketball team is a very good player,*" then you don't have a very good column idea. That is more of a feature story idea. That does not mean, however, that the senior guard from the local high school basketball team cannot be the topic of a column. Chances are, this particular athlete could be the jumping off point for a very good column. It's the point of the column that needs to be redefined. All you have to do is . . .

6. Give your column a human element. Let's go back to the senior guard on the local high school basketball team. You have observed her extraordinary hustle. She has both grace and strength. Her teammates look up to her and also genuinely like her. Best of all, she has shown over the past three seasons a great desire to win but the ability to handle a loss with dignity. She is a great example of what a high school athlete should strive to be. It dawns on you. That's the point of my column: *"This girl represents the best of high school sports"*. In this way, you've chosen a broader issue—*"Why high school sports can still be valuable".* Plus, you've given the idea a human element—a face and a name—that the readers will have an easier time relating to.

7. Reporting backs up your opinion. A person's opinion has credibility when it is considered valuable, informed and trustworthy. For a sports columnist to have any real impact, they must prove themselves to have credibility with their audience. The top sports columnists around the United States have immediate credibility because it is *their* opinion. Even if a reader does not agree with someone like the *Detroit Free Press'* Mitch Albom, or *Sports Illustrated's* Rick Reilly, they understand these writers have earned the right to be considered experts because of their experience, exposure and the superior style and craftsmanship they display in their work. Many columnists across the country—whether they write for 2,000,000 or 20,000 people—can claim this badge of credibility. To their readership they have demonstrated they know what they are talking about.

So how does a young or inexperienced columnist make his or her sports column credible? By remembering that, **good reporting is the basis of a good column.**

- Interview people that have first-hand knowledge of the column's topic.
- Since you will be stating an opinion, talk to people that you think will agree with your opinion. Find out why they feel the way they do; what has led them to their opinions.
- Talk to people who disagree with your opinion. It is especially valuable to find out why *they* feel the way they do and what has led them to *their* opinions.

By talking to people on both sides of an issue, you will learn more about the issue. This will lead to greater confidence and certainty that you actually know what you're talking about. It will also show the reader that you investigated the situation. That doesn't mean everyone will agree with you but most people—if they know you did your homework—will at least accept that your opinion is credible.

8. Take a stand. Once you have refined your column idea (you know what your point is) and you are convinced it is an issue that concerns your readers, you have to make sure you get your point across. Take a stand and **make it clear what you believe.** You don't want readers to have to guess at the point of a sports column. Wishy-washy columns don't appeal to anyone. It's better to make people mad than to leave no impression at all.

Two Approaches to Writing a Column: The Hammer and the Velvet Glove

As the names suggest, the Hammer and the Velvet Glove are two very different ways to take a stand and get a point across in a sports column. Again using the topic *"High school sports still have value"* with the standout girls' basketball player as the prime example, let's take a look at how the two different approaches would tackle the same subject.

The **Hammer** approach is hard and direct. The sports columnist's opinion—their stand—is driven home right in the first paragraph. *This young basketball player represents all that's good about high school sports and we should learn from her.* The rest of the column is spent nailing down all the reasons why this opinion has merit—her hustle, her grace, her sportsmanship. Any counter-arguments that can be anticipated are knocked away with just as much force. The sports columnist pounds away. All of the solid pieces of reporting, experience and expertise that have been gathered together build into one strongly made opinion.

The **Velvet Glove** is softer and often indirect. The sports columnist grabs the reader by the hand and gently guides them through the information. *Let me introduce you to a young basketball player I think you might like.* Often in this approach a sports columnist will use questions designed to make the reader think about the issue. When talking about the young girl's sportsmanship, the columnist might ask, *Can you think of any pro athletes who could learn from her?* Facts, impressions and comments gained through the reporting process are slowly added to the mix until a complete picture of this girl's personality and athletic skills has been painted. As the column nears its end, chances are the readers have reached the same conclusion as the sports columnist and could probably write the final lines themselves: *This young girl represents all that's good about high school sports. We all could learn from her example.*

Of course there are a vast number of ways a writer can tweak the Hammer and Velvet Glove approaches. That's both the fun and the challenge of column writing. Often, columnists spring surprises on the reader. Perhaps in the example of the girls' basketball player, the columnist decides a better point to make is that girls—not just boys—can be our athletic role models. If that were the case, the columnist might withhold the fact that the player is a girl until later in the column. The columnist would make it clear that this was a player worth respecting as a role model for their talent, desire and sportsmanship. By the time the reader is told the player is a girl, the reader would have to admit that she is a role model.

It is my opinion that the more indirect Velvet Glove method is ultimately more effective—if it is done well. The Velvet Glove gives the reader the chance to think about the issue while the sports columnist leads them to an unmistakable point. The problem with the Velvet Glove approach is that it takes a higher level of writing skill. Because it is an indirect approach, it is different from most of the stories a beginning sportswriter will be working on.

A Summary of Column Writing Skills

More than any other style of sports writing, column writing is an acquired skill. It takes practice to become good at the various stages of preparing a column. The columnist has to take several steps before a good column is written.

- Coming up with a topic idea (often a difficult task for inexperienced writers)
- Defining the topic enough to be sure it can work
- Clearly defining what your point will be
- Doing the reporting work to provide the background and details that will make the topic important to your readers
- Actually writing a powerful story that can impact your audience

Then when the column is done, the columnist must do it all again, up to five times a week at large newspapers. Columnists need to have a huge supply of topic ideas. They also need to have a thick skin when it comes to criticism. When you decide to write a column, you have to understand that not everyone will agree with you. Those who do not agree may be rather harsh in their criticism of your work, especially if your column was critical to someone or something they feel passionately about. Your best defense will always be that your column is based on what you have learned by being a good reporter, and that your opinion is truly your own opinion and one you believe in.

Great column writers have an unusually gifted sense of how to use the English language for maximum effect. What is too often overlooked is that great column writers remember to do the same high level of reporting that first made them great sportswriters.

They search out new sources of information and keep in touch with trusted contacts in an effort to keep a steady supply of good column ideas flowing into their brain. They try new techniques and approaches in their reporting to give them different perspectives on events they may have witnessed many times.

It is through the use of finely honed reporting skills that columnists keep their well-written stories fresh, lively and accurate.

CHAPTER 11

Little Things Mean a Lot

You may have noticed that I have not, to this point, discussed the importance of using proper grammar in sports stories. Further, the necessity of correct spelling has only been emphasized as it relates to people's names.

It's time to make some things perfectly clear.

Grammar and spelling are extremely important to a sportswriter. Poorly worded sentences show a lack of respect for your job and for the reader. They can also be confusing. Misspelled words give the same effect. Sports writing is no different than a fifth-grade essay or a college term paper: Errors in grammar and spelling count against the author. In sports writing, or any form of journalism, it's not just your grade that is affected by these mistakes. It is your reputation that is injured.

When readers comes across a story full of grammatical and spelling mistakes, they are likely to ask a very valid question: "If this sportswriter can't take the time to spell words correctly and writes sentences that are incomplete and confusing, then why should I believe they can get the facts straight?"

Grammar Matters

I am not a grammarian (one who teaches grammar) nor am I going to pretend to be one. This book is intended to teach you how to adapt the basic tools of writing that you should already be learning in the classroom—which include spelling, grammar, and accurate language—to a specific skill called sports writing. I am trying to demonstrate how to sharpen these standard writing tools in such a way that you can use the tools to begin building a fun and exciting career as a sportswriter.

I offer a few suggestions called **Grammar Tips:**

1. Do your best to **learn the rules of grammar** during the course of your regular schoolwork.
2. **Practice good grammar.** Whenever you are writing—even if it's a secret note to friends—write in a grammatically correct way. If you keep a diary or journal, write your personal notes correctly. Try to speak in full, complete and descriptive sentences.
3. **Read your writing aloud.** This often will help you to catch a sentence that is not grammatically correct or is incomplete. It will also help with word choice and making your writing clear and easy to understand. Quite often it is easier to hear a mistake than it is to read one, especially if you are the person who wrote the mistake in the first place.
4. **Learn from your mistakes.** Trust me, incorrect grammar is sometimes very difficult to detect. Part of the reason is that incorrect grammar is such a part of everyday speech. You won't hear a mistake if it sounds normal or regular to your ears. Therefore, when a teacher or editor points out an error in grammar, learn from it. Find out what exactly makes the phrase or sentence incorrect, incomplete or confusing, then write the same thought correctly.

Spelling Matters

You do not have to be a perfect speller to be a sportswriter. You do, however, need to recognize the problem if you are a poor speller and then take every possible measure to correct your mistakes. Learn how to use a dictionary and make sure you have one handy, even if you're out of town while writing a story.

Many spelling mistakes can be corrected easily with the modern convenience of the "check spelling" programs that are virtually standard on any computer software designed for writing or publishing. Make sure you use the "check spelling" program. Any beginning journalist should make it a part of their standard routine to check the spelling as soon as the final version of the story is saved and *before* it is ever submitted to a copy editor or for publication.

It's important to remember that spell-check programs are very effective but only to a certain point. You should be concentrating while using any spell-check program. It is fairly easy to mouse-click "ignore" when you should have clicked "change" and corrected a mistake. Even worse is when you change a correctly spelled name into a similarly spelled word. This can easily happen with names, since many names closely resemble a word. For example, the computer would read the name "Towes" and would suggest a change to "tows."

Also, spell-check devices only highlight *misspelled* words. The software won't catch the common mistakes of misusing words that sound alike but are spelled differently and have different meanings, like using "too" when you meant to write "two," or "their" when it should have been "there," and so on. Spell-check also won't catch typing mistakes that end up in correct words, like "hoe" when you meant to write "how," "the" when it should have been "they," or "its" when it should have been "it's."

That's why a sportswriter should always carefully read a completed story, making sure they are focused on trying to catch mistakes and improve the work instead of congratulating themselves for a job well done.

Remember to double-check hard to spell names, either with your own notes or a media guide. Pay close attention to any statistical figures in your story. You are a lot more likely to catch a typing mistake in your football story that turned 122 yards into 222 yards than any copy editor is.

The Value of Copy Editors

A copy editor is someone whose job is to read and check stories written by other people. It is their job to search for mistakes in grammar and spelling, as well as being on the lookout for factual errors or inconsistencies. Ideally, the copy editor also helps to improve a story's flow and rhythm and to insure that the important details are in their best locations. When you get to a newspaper of any size, someone else will be reading your story in the role of copy editor. At smaller papers, it will quite likely be the sports editor who has this responsibility, which means it is one of many tasks the sports editor has to perform on deadline in addition to designing the look of the paper and writing the headlines. Sometimes other sportswriters fill this role. Sports editors and sportswriters can be good copy editors, particularly when it comes to content, but larger papers will have people who do little else except edit stories. Usually full-time copy editors are excellent judges of a story's strengths and weaknesses and can be extremely helpful.

Copy editors can be valuable resources. Good copy editors can really improve a story. They will catch a phrase that doesn't explain a point well enough, or notice when a point was not given enough emphasis. They will also catch spelling and grammar mistakes and go a long way in making your story a polished piece. Really good copy editors also have a great wealth of knowledge about the local sports scene. Working with you to insure accuracy, a good copy editor can sometimes add some powerful background detail to a story.

Copy editors are not, however, a perfect solution to your problems. Copy editors are human, too. If they have already read a dozen game stories in one sitting, they might not be fresh enough to perform up to their capabilities. If they have another dozen stories waiting for them, they'll have to read your story quickly. Occasionally they will want to change your story in a way you disagree with and then you will have to be firm if you believe your own words are best.

Remember, copy editors work on a deadline, too. If a copy editor has to spend several minutes fixing mistakes in grammar and spelling that the sportswriter should not be making, then they are sacrificing some of the time that could have been spent really improving the story's content and composition.

Instead, their attitude will slip and their attention span will wane as they try desperately just to finish correcting all of your careless mistakes. If you keep giving them sloppy, amateurish stories, they'll probably consider you hopeless and never give you the full amount of help they are capable of giving.

A copy editor expects to be reading a final story, not a rough or first draft. **Good copy editors do their best work on clean copy.** If your stories are free of excessive errors in grammar and spelling, then the copy editor can focus on how the story reads. Then they can offer suggestions and ask pertinent questions that can truly give a story greater depth and more description, often through relatively minor changes.

Get the Facts Straight

I spent the better part of the second and third chapters discussing the importance of getting the facts and recognizing the difference between fact, opinion and fiction. I just want to take a little time to re-emphasize the importance of making sure the facts you present in your stories are accurate, paying special attention to the many references to statistics and names that fill most sports stories.

Statistics are, for most sports fans, a great part of sports. It's our own language. Baseball fans the world over know there's a huge difference between an earned run average of 2.45 and 5.42. This isn't just the difference of a couple of numerals being switched. Why, it's the difference between a Pedro Martinez and an anonymous middle relief pitcher.

Perhaps you've already figured out what I'm about to say: Just one digit out of place (or one digit deleted or added) can sometimes make a big difference, whether we're talking about a baseball player's batting average, the height or weight of a football player, or how much money a top tennis star made last year.

There are very few things worse than reading your own story in the next day's newspaper only to discover that you have given some kid the wrong number of points or made a mistake on which kid was the sixth relief pitcher in a game. One thing worse is receiving a call from an angry parent or coach who tells you what a rotten sportswriter you are because of your mistake. It really only takes one phone call of that variety to learn that people are reading your stories very closely and they expect you to get it right.

Don't laugh. This stuff happens, particularly at newspapers where high school sports are regularly covered, since the change in high school rosters is substantial with each passing season. I should know. I've made my share of mistakes that could have been easily avoided if I had double-checked my notes or a game program or taken the time to ask a simple question.

Here are two examples of mistakes that stick with me to this day, several years after the mistakes appeared on the harsh reality of the printed page.

1. **Get the uniform numbers right.** I notice that a high school football team's offensive line is dominating the game. Since linemen are too often overlooked, I make it a point to get the starters' numbers and positions. I decide that the left guard, No. 78, and the left tackle, No. 79, deserve special mention by name in the story. I look at my pre-printed roster, find numbers 78 and 79, and then read across to get the names. But I'm in a hurry, my eye wanders and what I'm actually reading are the names of No. 79 and No. 80. My intentions were good (to give some usually overlooked kids some deserved publicity), my observation was valid (the two players did have excellent games) but my execution stunk because I end-

ed up misidentifying the players. If I'd just taken a second look at the roster and double-checked, I probably would have seen my mistake. If I had thought to ask the coach about the two linemen, he would have mentioned their names and that too would have tipped me off that I was making a mistake. Since I didn't do those things, I got a nasty phone call from the father of one of the players as my reward.

2. **A misspelled name can ruin an entire story.** I remember a story I wrote about an annual recreation basketball tournament in our area. It had been around for about 45 years and had become a legendary local event among the basketball players and fans because of the tiny gym and rugged, high-scoring games. Instead of doing the standard roundup of that evening's results, I decided to really dig in and do a lot of extra work to produce a top-notch feature story that described what this tournament was all about. I interviewed about 10 people, including several older men who came almost every night to watch the players, tell stories, and enjoy each other's company. Most of them had been athletes who had gone on to coach or officiate sports. I really felt I had captured the event's unique spirit, particularly through the words of an extremely well-known and respected local golf professional named Tony Loch (rhymes with dock, spelled like Loch Ness Monster). He had played in the tournament when he was a young man, had watched his sons play in the tournament, and now came nearly every night as a fan. I was really proud of the story. My editor liked it. I was thinking about submitting it to writing competitions. Three hours after that day's paper had gone to press my editor realized I had spelled the golf pro's name wrong. My sports editor was apologetic for not catching the mistake but it wasn't his fault. The blame rested solely with the writer in this case. Since I had met and interviewed him many times before, I had not asked him to spell his name that night in the gym. I blew it. I spelled his name L-O-C-K-E throughout the whole story instead of the correct spelling of L-O-C-H. A great story had suddenly turned into a great, big mistake.

The Readers Know the Score

Have you ever watched an NFL game and heard the ex-jock announcer butcher a player's name? Even worse is when the out-of-touch TV guy misidentifies who made a crushing tackle or a key catch. How do you feel when the announcer doesn't have a clue who Number 54 is so he just says, "Number 54 just made a heck of a play right there!"?

It doesn't happen often but when it does, the mistake is glaring enough to make the knowledgeable sports fan yell at the ex-jock announcer, "I could do a better job than you're doing, you big, dumb goofball."

Chances are, the knowledgeable sports fan really could not do a better job. The sports fan does, however, have every right to expect the professional to do a better job.

It's the same for readers of newspapers, whether they're reading a major metropolitan daily paper that is covering their beloved Dallas Cowboys or a small-town paper that covers 10 high schools. **Readers expect a sportswriter's reporting to be accurate and they demand the sportswriter knows who the players are.**

Reporters usually don't know who *all* the players are when they show up at a game. When it comes to high school sports coverage, sportswriters will probably only know and recognize a few players on any given team. Fortunately, figuring out who the rest of the people are is not hard (thank goodness for uniform numbers). It just takes the proper preparation.

The sportswriter must be prepared to acquire the rosters for both teams at each event they cover. If it's a high school game that will often mean you need to copy the names and numbers down yourself out of the official scorebook. Try your best to find out the key players from each team before the game starts. As I talked about in **Chapter 6: Games Stories,** it is really beneficial to arrive 30 minutes early to a game.

Knowing Who's Who from each team (and making sure Who is spelled W-H-O and not H-O-O) is absolutely essential.

Once the game starts, sportswriters who cover high school sports—which means almost every sportswriter who is just starting out—have to be extra careful while taking their notes because:

- High school scorekeepers are not professional statisticians. Quite often they are just high school kids who are checking out the girl or guy across the gym or still worrying about the third question on today's pop quiz.
- You only have one chance to see the action. If you missed a basket, goal, or penalty when it happened, you won't get to see it on replay to figure out what happened. In 15 years of covering high school sports, I have never seen a TV monitor installed for the purpose of allowing the press to watch instant replays. Sportswriters covering major college and professional events usually have the advantage of being able to view a replay of important plays, since most of those games are being televised

and it is quite common for larger press boxes to have televisions.
- Most importantly, you have to keep your own statistics.

In **Chapter 6: Game Stories,** I laid out a few of the ground rules of keeping your own statistics. It is something that you will have to learn how to do and you will need to learn how to do it accurately and quickly.

A good way to practice your note taking is to watch a game on television and take notes. I would suggest turning the sound off. That way you are completely reliant on your own skills. Do this a couple of times, particularly if you are just learning to take notes, trying to change the way you take notes, or are adding a new element to your scorekeeping system. Better to make a bunch of mistakes while practicing than when it's really your responsibility to get it right.

It is ironic that the sportswriters who have advanced to the point where they are covering major college and professional sports—presumably because they were the best sportswriters available—are now afforded the luxury of being handed every conceivable statistic before, during, and after a game. It's my observation that most of these sportswriters still keep their own statistical notations during a game. What I have done when I'm covering college or pro games is to alter my note-taking style a bit. Basically, I streamline the notes. I still want a framework of what happened in the game but I'm not that concerned about accounting for every statistical detail. You may have noticed that the example of my notes for a college football game shown in **Figure 4** (Chapter 3) differs quite a bit from my high school football notes shown in **Figure 12** (Chapter 6). When I know that the full and complete statistics will be provided to me after a game, I try to focus more on the broader happenings in a game.

An Example of Different Note-Taking Styles

At a college football game where I'll get a 10-page "stats package" I might watch only a certain offensive lineman for a few plays in a row if I think that person is a key to the game or because I'm planning on writing either a sidebar or feature story about him. I want to see how he plays his position, whether he emphasizes strength or technique and whether he is dominating or adequate. Chances are, while I'm isolating on this one player, I might not be completely sure who carried the ball, especially if the play goes away from the lineman I'm watching. I'm basically giving up some information at that moment to get some other information that I think will be important and interesting to a story. I can do this because I know that if I need to find out who carried the ball on a certain play I can always refer to the stats package. Also, if I see someone in the stands that I think I should interview (a player's parent, a school official, an NFL scout), I can go do it right then knowing that all of the statistical information I'll miss will still be available for me.

These are things you have to be careful about doing at high school games. If you want to focus on an offensive lineman, you will still need to get the basics of the play recorded. If you want to interview someone, you should try to do it during halftime. You have to be ready to account for every single yard gained or lost, whether it's a thrilling last-minute victory or one of those lopsided 40-0 contests where the third- and fourth-string running backs get to carry the football. You do this because if you happen to stop paying attention for a couple of Johnny Smith's carries you could end up crediting him with 98 yards rushing when he really gained 103 yards. You keep paying attention, keep taking careful statistical notes because first and foremost you have respect for yourself and your profession and you want to be as accurate as you possibly can. You also do not want to have Johnny Smith's mom on the phone the next day telling you what a lousy reporter you are because you didn't credit her son for that all-important 100-yard game. Now it may be true that Mrs. Smith could benefit from a little bit of professional counseling but she has made an important point painfully clear: Little things mean a lot.

Some More Things that Matter

I'd like to take a few minutes to run down some other things that will matter when you actually start writing sports stories for a newspaper, whether it's your school's four-page photo-copied weekly or as a recent college graduate taking your first "real" job.

- **Learn how to use a camera.** Sports are about action and as much as a sportswriter would like to believe otherwise, there's nothing quite like a great sports picture to interest readers in a story. Photographs are an essential part of any sports section. Great action photos are difficult to take and few people will expect a sportswriter to take great photos. Being able to snap a posed picture, however, is really not that difficult and can often be quite useful. Considering that your first real job will probably be at a smaller newspaper, they will love the fact that you can handle simple photo assignments by yourself. Some weekly and small daily newspapers require reporters to take their own pictures and depend on them for the photographs that will run in a sports section. Knowing how to use a camera could give you an edge over other job applicants. Owning your own camera is a real plus. Who knows? With practice you might actually learn to take that top-notch action photo.

- **Never forget that you are an objective reporter.** Sportswriters attend games and practices and interview people because that is their job. They are not there to root for a certain team or to become best friends with a coach or player. You should be respectful and you can certainly be friendly but you can't let your personal feelings for a particular team or individual cloud your judgment of what took place in a game. Take the time to get perspective and comments from both the winning and the losing team or players whenever possible.
- **The press box is for the press,** not for your buddies, wives/husbands, girlfriends/boyfriends, or your children. Respect your job and your fellow sportswriters and leave everyone else at home. If you want to show your friends or family where you work, bring them around for introductions before the game starts and then buy them a ticket in the stands. The reason you do this is because of one of the oldest rules of sports writing: "There is no cheering in the press box." This is a time-honored rule and it relates directly to the need to remain objective. Bring someone who is not a member of the working press into a press box and it's only a matter of time before they are cheering (or jeering) and generally distracting the people who are trying to work. Plus, they'll end up eating the free food we sportswriters depend on.
- **Remember who you are writing for.** Who are your readers? Which team are they interested in? Sportswriters should frame their stories around the team that is important to their readers. When I covered the University of New Hampshire football team, the lead and emphasis of my game stories always centered on what happened to UNH. If UNH won by 20 points, I explained why it was the superior team. If it lost the game by 20 points then I emphasized *why UNH was beaten.* I tried to remain objective by talking with the opposing coach and players and noting what they did well and what they did poorly. If the opposing team had particular players who were significant to

the outcome, I made sure to mention their contribution but they never became the emphasis of the story. Even when UNH lost by 20 points and didn't have a single noteworthy performance, I made sure my story reflected the game from UNH's perspective because that was the team my readers were concerned about.

- **Learn how to type—fast and accurately.** Speed is important when it comes to sports writing, especially since so many games are played at night and have to be written in time to appear in the next day's morning newspapers. Being able to use all of your fingers while typing and to have it be second nature is a great benefit when it comes to deadline writing. All it probably takes is a couple of typing classes to teach you the proper finger placement on a keyboard and then the willingness to keep at it through the initial couple of stories when it feels very awkward. Your speed will increase quite naturally, especially since a full-time sportswriter is routinely writing a couple of stories a day. If you are starting your career as a free-lancer, take my advice. Do not submit a hand-written story to the sports editor. That might be the end of your career right then.

CHAPTER 12

It's Sports Business Now

There's no sense in trying to deny it or escape it. Sports are big, big, big business. Money matters.

- Money often means the difference between winning and losing.
- Money eventually determines whether the star player stays in town.
- Money is the ultimate consideration of whether a team—even a league—remains in operation.

The higher the sportswriter goes on the sports food chain, the more he or she will have to deal with issues that revolve around money.

It used to be that the most important numbers associated with a professional athlete were his uniform number and his statistical averages. Now the one number that really matters is an athlete's salary. It defines the athlete's worth and often decides whether they will stay with a team or play somewhere else the next season. Increasingly, good players are being traded or released because they have priced themselves out of a particular club's budget and are replaced by marginal or untested players who are less expensive to employ.

In today's wacky sports business world, a second baseman who hits .250 is considered a bargain at $1 million a year.

Money is central to just about every aspect of professional and even major college sports. How much do tickets cost? What does it cost to take a family of four to a game? Will the city pay for a new stadium to keep a pro football/baseball/hockey team from moving to a new city? Is a shortstop, any shortstop, worth $25 million a season? Can major league baseball teams in smaller cities like Kansas City make enough money to compete against the super-rich clubs in major cities like New York? Will enough people watch the new women's professional soccer teams to secure a TV contract that is needed to insure enough money to keep the league going? Will the college give its football coach a huge raise? Can the college afford to keep all of its sports programs? Are coaches of women's college teams paid the same as coaches for men's college teams?

These are questions that are asked, addressed and puzzled over every single day across the country. The huge amount of media that covers sports has become a business monster in itself. There are sports sections in thousands of newspapers, hundreds of specialty sport magazines, local, regional and national sports Web sites, television and radio sports reports. As if that wasn't enough to satisfy our desire for sports, there are an ever-greater number of broadcast hours devoted to the mostly mindless chatter that goes under the heading of "Sports Talk."

All of these media options use sports as a means to generate money for their respective companies or individual owners.

Long gone are the days of sports idols playing for the love of the game. They may still love playing the game but they play for much more than just love. They are playing for the money they make—money for themselves, for their schools or employers, even for those sportswriters and sportscasters who are up in the press box.

Think about this next statement seriously. *If you want to cover people who love the game and that's the only reason they play it, then you better accept that you will be writing about the local town recreation league teams.*

Even the high school scene has been significantly influenced by the power of money. The lure of a college scholarship has contributed to a rapid increase in out-of-school competition and single-sport specialization at an early age and has thus changed the youth sports landscape dramatically over the past 15 years. Increasingly, a young athlete has to spend extraordinary amounts of time and money as part of a special club (soccer, basketball, gymnastics, skiing, etc.) just to have a competitive chance at making the varsity team. Athletes and their parents are investing large amounts of time and money into sports careers before the athletes are even teenagers.

Whether it's spent or earned, money has dramatically altered the sports landscape over the past quarter-century and it's important that future sportswriters understand that.

Preparing for a Sports Writing Career

Sports writing is an exciting career path for a sports enthusiast to pursue. If anything, the increase in media options (Web sites, cable television, specialty magazines) has opened up even more job possibilities in the sports writing profession. Below are answers to some questions you might have about sports writing as a career.

Do I Need a Journalism Degree?

In a word, No, but . . . earning a journalism degree is a good idea and it is a course of study offered at many colleges (and is often offered in high school). One of the best aspects of being in a journalism degree program is that many colleges set up their students with summer jobs, called internships, at newspapers where the students get great practical experience as a reporter.

Journalism school is an excellent place to learn about the theories and the ethics of reporting. Yes, even reporters have rules of conduct and behavior.

If you are serious about journalism you should work for the college newspaper, even if there are no openings in the sports department (the same is true at the high school level). This will go a long way toward teaching you about the importance of meeting deadlines, working under pressure, and accepting some of the responsibilities of the job.

Most importantly, the combination of your college classes and practical work experience will probably give you a very good idea of whether this is truly a profession that you want to pursue.

Besides Journalism Courses, What Else Should I Study?

While you're in college, make every effort to take some business classes, specifically sports business courses if they are offered. As I stressed in the beginning of this chapter, sports are business and athletes, coaches and owners are, to varying degrees, businesspeople. Learn how marketing and promotions are as important to the success of a professional or major college sports team as the win-loss record.

A few classes in contract law would probably be helpful, as would courses that discuss the process and the history of relations and negotiations between labor and management. In the world of sports, the players are the labor, which essentially means the employees. The owners, leagues, and colleges fall under the heading of management, meaning the employers. Labor-management relations were critical and often extremely tense issues in professional sports in the last quarter of the 20th century. The NFL, NBA, NHL, and Major League Baseball all had work stoppages when either the players went on strike or the owners shut the league down while contract negotiations stalled. The World Series was even canceled in 1994. The issues of money—who has it, how will it be shared, how will it be spent and how much is too much—are not going to disappear any time in the near future. A beat writer covering a professional football team will end up writing more business stories than feature stories if the owner starts making noise about moving the franchise.

Should I Only Write Sports Stories?

No. The more experience you can get within the structure of a newspaper, the better your overall reporting skills will be. Also, you'll have a better grip on the entire newspaper business and how sports fit into the total package. Plus, your reporting will be sharpened and your writing tested by purposely working on stories that are "outside the sports box."

Once you feel like you know how to report and write a business story, then you better start learning how to report and write a crime story. Probably the best thing a young sportswriter could do while in college is to get an internship covering the cops, courts and politicians for a local daily newspaper. Why?

Sooner or later in this profession the criminal misdeeds of a local athlete or coach, whether at the professional, college or high school level, will be something you will have to report on and write about. If you have already acquired the skills and basic awareness of how to research court documents, how to work through the chain of command at a police station, and how to get information from someone who is absolutely opposed to talking to you, then you will have an edge on all the other young or inexperienced sportswriters.

Two good reasons for sportswriters to be able to act like crime reporters:

- **Athletes get in legal trouble.** Their status as celebrities—highly paid celebrities in many cases—means their legal problems will be news stories that a sportswriter should be willing and able to write.
- **Experience as a "real news" reporter is the surest way to learn how to be a good reporter.** If you can sort out the true story after talking to police officers, lawyers, politicians, and criminals, then writing an accurate sports story will be relatively easy.

Can Women and Minorities Be Sportswriters?

Yes, though it really wasn't that long ago where a more factual and realistic answer would have been "No." In the mid-1960s, sports writing reflected most of American society. It was dominated and controlled by white males. This is probably one of the most positive trends in the field over the past 20 to 30 years. Women and minority sportswriters are now working for some of the most prestigious and largest newspapers in the country, adding important and needed voices to America's sports pages.

Women and minority sportswriters are still, however, a relatively small percentage of the total working population.

Are There any Sports I Should Shy Away from Covering?

Absolutely not. Every new sport is an eye-opening experience. There are several good reasons to actually request covering events that are out of the ordinary or unfamiliar to you.

Advantages to new sports:

- Covering a new sport with unfamiliar people gives you a hands-on refresher course in the fundamentals of reporting. Any lazy habits you may have developed during routine, repetitious assignments will be apparent.
- New people present a great number of feature story ideas. Some of the best stories you'll ever write are going to be about people who are basically unknown to your reader. Remember: **Everybody has a story to tell.**

- You can quickly become your newspaper's expert on the new sport. This can open up some significant career opportunities if you are willing to work hard. Consider this. Twenty years ago stock car racing, what we know as Winston Cup, was essentially a sport given large amounts of coverage only in the Southeast. Now it has gone national and most large newspapers, not to mention the many specialty magazines, have full-time auto racing writers. Writers who got in on the ground floor of this now huge sporting enterprise have done quite well for themselves. If I were to guess, someone who is adept and willing to write about the so-called Extreme or Action Sports (skateboarding, snowboarding, rock climbing, etc.) can carve out a lucrative career covering sports that just a few years ago would have been scoffed at in most sports departments.

Do I Have What it Takes to be a Sports Writer?

Of course, that's a question that ultimately you will have to answer—or maybe your first editor will end up answering for you. There's no magic formula for figuring out who will be an average sportswriter, who will be good, and who will be superior. Further, you will have to find out what level of sports you like to cover and be associated with. Perhaps, you will aspire to cover the largest and most important events in the world—the Super Bowl, the Olympics, the World Series. Maybe you want to prove yourself as a superior writer and become a columnist. Or, you may discover you want to be a beat writer covering major college basketball because you love the raw energy of a student-based crowd and the yearly possibility that the local team will go to the NCAA tournament. Perhaps you will find that you want to keep a broad mix of sports on your computer screen because you appreciate the relative innocence of high school sports but enjoy having the responsibility of being a beat writer for the local college football team. I've known people who work as sportswriters strictly on a part-time basis. They do it because they love the games, like talking to people and enjoy the challenge of crafting a descriptive and readable story.

If you're still in middle school, go to a friend's game and write a story about it. Try to practice the fundamentals I have talked about. Get a list of players from both teams. Introduce yourself to the coaches and tell them what you're doing. Pay attention during the game. Take notes in a neat, orderly fashion that allows you to know how every player has done, not just your buddy. Talk to the coaches and a couple of friends after the game and try to accurately use their comments. You can also practice your craft by writing stories from the games that you watch on television. Then compare your story to one written in the local newspaper or available on a Web site from that team's hometown newspaper.

If you're in high school, then join the school newspaper and accept regular assignments. Try to think up story ideas on your own. Work on writing stories in the different styles discussed in chapters 6-10 (game story, feature story, sidebar, notebook, and column). If you are finding that this is something you really enjoy doing and are willing to accept the responsibility, seek out the sports editor of your local newspaper and see if you can get a part-time job or an internship.

In college seek out the editors at the school newspaper and the local newspaper. Both will probably need extra help. Prove to them that you will work hard, that you'll accept criticism and then improve your work, and that you can be counted on to turn in a story *on time* with the fundamental details and important information.

Whatever your age or your experience, be sure to remember that there's more to sports writing than just sports and writing. There is always the critical, most important job of being a reporter. You are there to get the facts and to get them straight.

It is through reporting that you can really get into the heart of this game called being a sportswriter and it is because of your reporting that you can stay in the game as long as you want.

Each of us is different and we each have different goals in life. Still, if you enjoy writing about sports and have proven you have the ability and dedication to be a sportswriter, you probably share some common traits.

Some of What it Takes to be a Sportswriter

1. A desire to be around people and to talk with people
2. An understanding and appreciation of language
3. A desire to write
4. A passion for sports
5. Experience

Start writing now and keep on writing.

To view our other titles and
to order more copies of

Sports Writing
A BEGINNER'S GUIDE

visit our website at

www.discoverwriting.com

Phone: 1-800-613-8055 • Fax: 1-802-897-2084

Or mail in the form below with your check, credit card or purchase order.

METHOD OF PAYMENT: ☐ Check or money order enclosed ☐ Purchase order attached P.O.#_____

☐ Mastercard   ☐ Visa

Signature_____

Credit Card#_____ Exp.Date_____

PLEASE PRINT

NAME _____ HOME PHONE _____

HOME ADDRESS _____

CITY _____ STATE _____ ZIP CODE _____

TITLE	PRICE	QTY	AMOUNT
SPORTS WRITING - A BEGINNER'S GUIDE	$15.00		
Shipping & Handling $5.95 plus $1 for ea. additional item			
VT Residents add 6%			
Make check payable to: DWC, P.O. Box 264, Shoreham, VT 05770	**TOTAL**		